D0378329

Compass &
Map Navigator

Help Us Keep This Guide Up to Date

Every effort has been made by the author and editors to make this guide as accurate and useful as possible. However, many things can change after a guide is published—new products and information become available, regulations change, techniques evolve, etc.

We would love to hear from you concerning your experiences with this guide and how you feel it could be improved and be kept up to date. While we may not be able to respond to all comments and suggestions, we'll take them to heart and we'll also make certain to share them with the author. Please send your comments and suggestions to the following address:

The Globe Pequot Press
Reader Response/Editorial Department
P.O. Box 480
Guilford, CT 06437
Or you may e-mail us at:
editorial@globe-pequot.com

Thanks for your input, and happy travels!

Compass & Map Navigator

The Complete Guide to Staying Found

New Revised Edition

By Michael Hodgson

Illustrated by Jon Cox

Foreword by Lou Whittaker

Distributed by

The
Globe
Pequot
Press

Guilford, Connecticut

Copyright 1997, 2000 by Michael Hodgson

Cover design by Brendon Weaver
Cover photo by Darwin Wigget/Deborah Sussex, Courtesy NOLS
Text design by Lisa Reneson

Library of Congress Cataloging-in-Publication Data
Hodgson, Michael.
    Compass and map navigator: the complete guide to staying
found/by Michael Hodgson.-- New revised edition
        p. cm.
    Includes bibliographical references.
    ISBN 0-7627-0488-8
    1. Map reading. 2. Navigation. I. Title.

GA151 .H57 2000
796.5--dc21   00-041724

Distributed by the Globe Pequot Press
Manufactured in the United States of America
New Revised Edition/Fourth Printing

To Johnny "the-man-the-myth-the-legend" Dodd, Beth Howard, Dan Glick, and Roy Wallack—my Eco-Challenge teammates, who helped guide my soul while I guided their steps.

Contents

Foreword

Proper preparation for your time in the outdoors is necessary for a successful outing. It doesn't take a huge commitment in time or money, but rather a dedication to be responsible for yourself and for the time and feelings of others. An obvious case in point are the many rescue missions I have been involved in on Mt. Rainier—a mountain I have lived with and learned from since my childhood. We have found climbers, who were familiar with the mountain and who had previous climbing experience, face down on the flat open slopes of the mountain. No avalanches, no falls, just lying there. Many others are lost and may never be found. I have asked myself again and again, what makes experienced climbers lose their way or just lay down and say "I give up?" The weather closes in and they don't have the equipment or the training to cope with the panic that ends their lives. The cost for these rescue efforts is substantial in both time and money, but the cost in lives is more than can be determined. The sad thing is that as more and more people come into the outdoors, more and more come unprepared.

I have been climbing with my brother Jim, since I was a teenager, and have led expeditions to Kangchenjunga, Everest, and K2. With us on every one of these expeditions was a compass and our knowledge of how to use it. The skills I have learned over my many years of climbing have not only allowed me to explore many of the world's most remote areas and highest peaks, but also to get me back down and home safely. After all, getting to the top is only half the trip.

Today, my company, Rainier Mountaineering Inc., guides clients to all corners of the world and prepares and trains them in basic survival skills, which include map and compass. We also take kids from the local schools out for one-day hikes and teach them not only map and compass, but skills that one day may be called upon to save their lives. A company like mine doesn't become so successful without having a sound knowledge in how to train and protect their clients.

Read and enjoy this book. More importantly, however, embrace the knowledge and understanding of the simple, yet potentially lifesaving, skills it imparts. As I said, I have been climbing and guiding for over sixty years and plan to do so for some time to come. With proper preparation, so should you.

Lou Whittaker

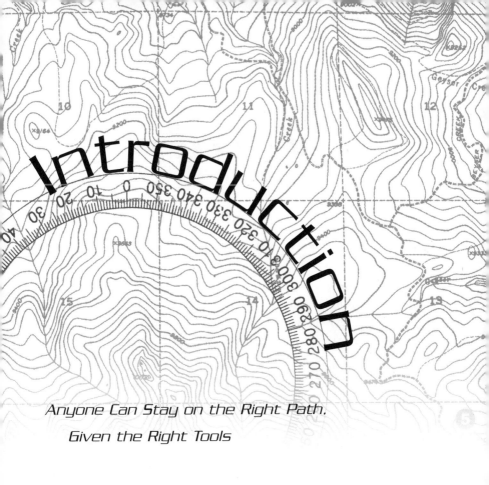

Introduction

Anyone Can Stay on the Right Path,
Given the Right Tools

Introduction

Anyone Can Stay on the Right Path, Given the Right Tools

Which way!? Our team of journalists, competing in the first Eco-Challenge (a 360-mile, nonstop adventure race by foot, paddle, mountain bike, and climbing rope), stood on top of a ridge, gazing across a jumbled landscape of rocks and canyons, The faint tracks before us could be trails or just tracks from others who had gotten lost. Other teams milled about in a confused fashion. We had all hiked 70 miles across some very unforgiving desert terrain in just under a day and a half. Many of us were almost out of water. A few of the teams had members who appeared to be on the verge of collapse.

I tried to block out the distractions and focus on the task at hand—getting us on the right path and to the next water hole before we all ran dry. As the team navigator, the pressure rested squarely on my shoulders. The sun began to set, washing out essential features and details on the landscape. I had to work quickly.

Taking mental pictures of the landscape, I tucked shapes away into my mind for future reference. Then I shot several key bearings with my compass and plotted a course. The path that became clear to me headed in a direction that appeared to make no logical sense—unless you factored in all the bits of information available. I headed off resolutely, although there was no denying the tiny lump in my throat . . . what if I were wrong? Every few hundred feet I glanced around, taking more mental pictures, comparing them with what I knew the map said, and placing us on the map accordingly.

A blanket of darkness wrapped around us, leaving me no choice but to work with silhouettes, my map and compass, and the stars above. One of my teammates, Johnny Dodd, told me to glance back up the trail. There, strung out behind me, were more than twenty-five bobbing headlamps, representing five other teams, I had become the Pied Piper, hopefully leading us all to life-sustaining water.

We came to a fork in the road and a debate ensued. Most of the footprints from previous teams headed to the right. My instincts and navigational information indicated that left was the correct choice. My team backed my choice so off we headed, with the other teams right behind. The night became an epic, with us arriving at the watering hole (I was correct) at 4:00 A.M. A number of other teams got hopelessly lost going through the same terrain—probably because they didn't have all the skills or experience they needed to see them through the navigational challenges. I managed to get us where we needed to be only because I studied every piece of the navigational puzzle before me and then fit each piece together until it made sense.

Why do people get lost? There are many reasons, and most of them are completely avoidable. The most common mistake is not packing a map and compass because you're "just going out for a quick hike on a clearly marked trail." All you have to do is be day-dreaming or chatting with your partners and you may walk off one trail and onto another, completely unaware. Another mistake is lack of preparation. Instead, the trip is on, so you grab a map, toss the compass in the pack, and go, with no forethought or proper map homework. I always study my maps before I go out, which is why I probably have an easier time staying on course. Yet another reason is blindly trusting your partner, who may be just as hope-lessly lost as you. Everyone who wants to safely enjoy the great outdoors should master basic navigational skills and be able to use them.

Having been a member of several search and rescue teams and also a professional mountain guide, I am continually amazed by the number of people I encounter who dutifully carry along a map and shiny new compass yet have absolutely no idea where they are, where they're heading, or where they came from. Sure, packing along a topographic map and a compass fulfill two of the "ten essentials" for safe backcountry travel, but what good are they if you don't know how to use them? Not much! You may as well pack a world atlas or road map, because without map and compass skills, a road map will be as good as a regular topographic map in the backcountry.

There's an art to staying found that involves using your head, remaining observant, and applying map and compass skills properly. The basic skills involved in simple navigation are not all that hard to acquire. What follows is a very easy-to-use guide to staying found. It includes illustrations and diagrams, courtesy of the folks at Brunton, to assist you in picking the right tools, learning how to use them, and staying on course.

With this book and a bit of practice, you'll soon be able to say with confidence that you, like the author (aka "navgod" to his friends and fellow adventure racing competitors), have never been lost—disoriented for a few days, maybe, but never lost.

Happy trails!

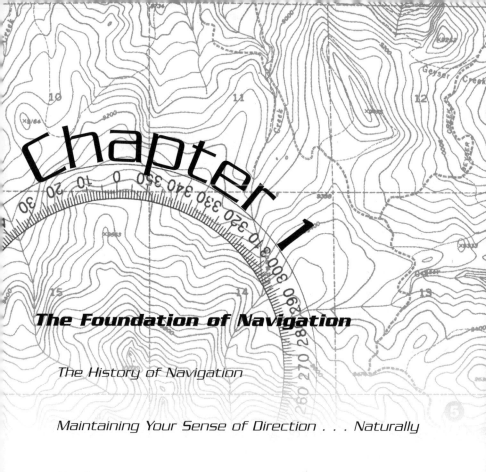

Chapter 1

The Foundation of Navigation

The History of Navigation

Maintaining Your Sense of Direction . . . Naturally

On Staying Found When You Suspect You're Lost

The Foundation of Navigation

The History of Navigation

Before the invention of the compass, early travelers and mariners navigated by the lay of the land as well as the positions of the sun and stars. The Vikings, possibly some of the greatest and most skilled adventurers of their time, relied completely on the position of the sun and stars to find their way across the ocean and back home again. Whenever these celestial bodies were obscured by fog or clouds, the Vikings simply drifted until the weather cleared.

Early Sumerians, Cretans, Egyptians, Phoenicians, Greeks, Romans, and Scandinavians navigated on the sea by hugging a coastline and identifying their position in relation to known objects on land. These mariners traveled by day and rested at night. None of them had maps or charts, although some relied on a list of directions that identified landmarks, anchorages, and hazards such as shoals and reefs.

Land explorers had both maps and lists. However, since few ventured far from home, the maps were useful only to armies and traders. The oldest known surviving maps come from Mesopotamia and are etched into clay tablets. Although there are references to older maps in Greek and Roman writings, these maps were drawn onto parchment paper and have since disappeared.

During the twelfth century the first crude compass was created. It resulted from the discovery that the magnetized iron found in lodestone would align itself in a north–south fashion if floated on a piece of wood in a container of water. Shortly thereafter, it was discovered that magnetizing an iron or steel needle would cause the needle, too, to align itself in a north–south fashion.

These compasses were used first by the Chinese and early explorers in European countries. The ability of the early compass designs, as well as today's modern versions, to function is due to the physical properties of the earth; it's really just a huge magnet. The earth's magnetic poles (or points of polarity) are oval areas located approximately 1,300 miles from the geographic North and South Poles. A magnetized needle simply aligns itself with the irregular lines of magnetic force that connect the north and south magnetic poles. In a few places on earth, the magnetic lines of force happen to match the meridians of geographic north and south. In most cases, however, the magnetic needle points a few degrees to the east or west of geographic (true) north. This is known as declination, which I will explain in detail later.

Despite the development of the compass, it wasn't until the late seventeenth century, when astronomical discoveries linked with mapmaking techniques allowed for the designation of lines of longitude, that maps began to come of age and navigation leapt forward. For the first time, the location of specific places was accurately determined and mapped. This led to increased accuracy in mapping coastlines on eighteenth-century maps.

During the nineteenth century land exploration began to explode as armies and teams of adventurers took off in earnest to claim places unknown (to them, at least) for king, queen, country, and their own glory. This exploration of continental interiors began to fill the voids in the maps. The scientific community was a driving force in the push to map distant lands; numerous scholarly and scientific studies of the earth were undertaken.

The real father of today's modern compass was David W. Brunton, who invented a device known as the Pocket Transit, a professional surveyor's instrument, in 1894 (Figure 1–1). Still, the principles of this instrument were the same as those used by the Chinese (who floated a magnetized needle on a straw or splinter of wood in a bowl of water) and by Arab mariners (who, it is reported, suspended a magnetized piece of iron from a piece of string). And believe it or not, the compasses you use today, although made of far more modern materials, rely on the same principles—a magnetized piece of metal is allowed to rotate freely in solution as it seeks magnetic field alignment.

Through the use of surveying tools and international cooperation, the twentieth century saw dramatic improvement in mapping coverage. Cooperative efforts, such as the joint venture between the United States and a number of Latin American governments dubbed the Inter-American Geodetic Survey, resulted in the production of more accurate maps for much of the Western Hemisphere by 1970.

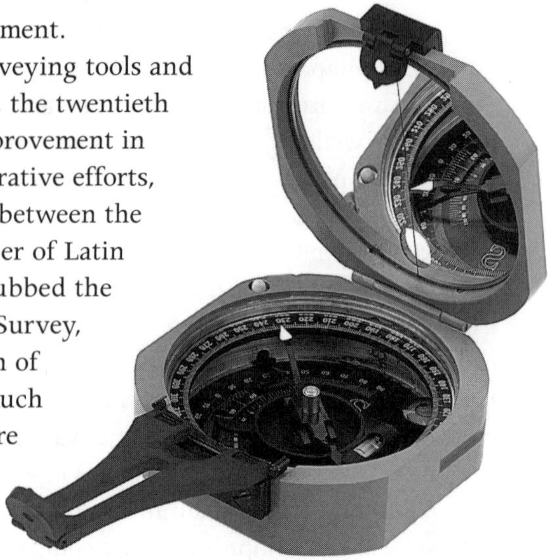

Still, not all of the world has been mapped, and some of what has been mapped has not been mapped very well. I was

Figure 1-1 Brunton Pocket Transit surveying compass. Developed by David Brunton, a mining engineer, and patented in 1894.

trekking in Baja a number of years back and became very confused trying to put together what the land and my eyes were telling me and what the Mexican-produced topographic map said I should be seeing. After much consternation and scouting, I came to realize that the mountain I was standing on was the one the map said was 10 miles distant, and the mountain I was looking at was, in fact, the mountain the map said I was standing on. A *major* 10-mile flipflop error by both a surveyor and a cartographer. Lesson: Never trust what a map has to say unless you can prove it through careful observation and compass use.

Maintaining Your Sense of Direction? . . . Naturally

While no one can honestly claim to have an infallible sense of direction, the key to staying found and knowing where you are most of the time is simply this: Stay alert to your surroundings. The best navigators stay on course by using their eyes, their ears, their noses, and their wits (as well as their knowledge of map and compass skills)—all in relationship with each other. My daughter Nicole often jokes that while I never seem to get lost when I'm outdoors, inside a mall I'm absolutely hopeless, and she's basically right. In a mall I tend to tune out and consequently remove myself from the changing pictures as I walk, setting myself up time and again to wonder, Where in the @#$% is the main entrance and where did I leave the car? If I would just take a lesson from my own words—stay alert—I might not face such urban challenges.

Accurate navigation begins with 360-degree awareness 100 percent of the time. Your eyes should always be searching, seeking clues to the course you're on. Pay close attention to trees, logs, rocks, hills, ridges, streams, and even man-made landmarks as you pass them. Make mental notes as you go. Look over your shoulder so that you can view how the features may change as you move along. When I taught advanced map and compass courses, most students worked on cruise control finding their way from point A to point B. Yet, if asked to try to head back the way they came and return to point A, they would invariably question themselves and the route. Why? Because what may seem intimately familiar going one way takes on an entirely different face from the other side. Get into the habit of looking forward, from side-to-side, and over your shoulder as you walk along (Figure 1-2).

Take note of your directional changes and associate them with the terrain surrounding you. Keep putting together, rather like assembling a puzzle, all the different features of the various landmarks you're passing. Continually ask yourself, If I had to return to where I started right now, how would I go? Although you may not be using a compass, try to think directionally. The hill you're going around right now lies to the east, while that tall pine standing out in the middle of the meadow ahead marks north. Keep track of all trail intersections, stream crossings, major elevation changes, and other significant features. Each piece you observe becomes a critical part of the entire picture you must assemble in order for you, and perhaps your group, to stay the course.

Don't forget to take the sky into account as well. Although the sun moves across the sky (as does the moon) as the earth spins, learning to associate times of day with the sun's position in relation

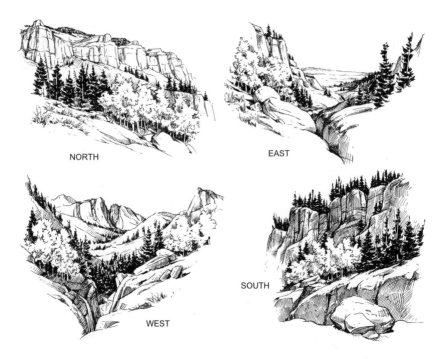

NORTH

EAST

SOUTH

WEST

Figure 1-2

to landmarks you're passing can be immensely helpful in determining where you are should you need to retrace your steps. Using the sun and a watch or even a stick in the ground to determine direction is also useful, as I'll demonstrate later in this book.

Navigation relies strongly on your ears and nose, too. You may not be able to see the stream, but if you can hear it, make a note where it lies and estimate how far away it is. If you drop into a valley and it feels far cooler than other valleys you've passed through that day, make a note. Perhaps you're walking through a grove of trees or across a meadow and notice a unique odor—the pungent aroma of wild onion or the scent of cedar. Make a mental note.

Using eyes, ears, and nose to stay on course is how pioneers and Native Americans successfully navigated terrain much wilder than it is now—all without the aid of a compass or map. You can do it, too, with a lot of practice.

On Staying Found When You Suspect You're Lost

It has been rumored that famed outdoorsman Daniel Boone was never lost, although he did admit to being "mighty disoriented for a week or two." In this day and age of search and rescue teams, maps, compasses, and high technology, *lost* most often means that you will be late for dinner. At worst it generally means that someone else will find you. The following are some tips aimed at helping you and your loved ones stay found:

❂ Always tell a family member or close friend where you're going, when you'll be leaving, and when you plan on returning—and then stick to your plan.

❂ Be prepared for the worst. Just because you're heading out for a day hike under sunny skies doesn't mean you won't be forced to spend a night out in adverse weather conditions. Extra food and clothing are a minimum must. Carry a lightweight survival kit with a space blanket, a plastic tarp, nylon cord, waterproof matches, a fire starter, a whistle, a signal mirror, water purification tablets, a metal cup in which to heat water, a small flashlight, and a knife.

❂ Don't just carry a map and compass; become proficient at using these tools. This book is an excellent place to begin your proficiency training, but reading alone won't do you much good. You must get out and practice, practice, practice. Joining an orienteering club near you or starting a map and compass club is a great way to gain experience and have a lot of fun.

❂ Pay attention to your surroundings. Staying on the correct path and then being able to find your way back again requires 360-degree observation. Make mental notes of landmarks as you're walking toward them and then as you're walking away from them.

❂ Should you get lost, don't panic. Recognize the problem and then rationally work your way through it. Most often, if you sit down and calmly reflect for a few minutes, mentally retracing your steps, the solution becomes clear.

✪ If you come to the conclusion that you're definitely lost, *stay put*! Although it's tempting to wander, there are numerous tales of lost individuals being found dead weeks or months after a search was begun, simply because they wandered out of the area where the search and rescue crew expected them to be.

✪ Drink plenty of water. Your body can do without food for a few days, but it cannot function without water.

✪ Signal your position by building a smoky fire.

✪ If you run out of food, don't eat anything unless you're sure you can identify it as edible.

✪ Shelter yourself from the elements as best you can. Use the tarp in your survival kit to fashion a lean-to. Use dry leaves and other dry plant debris (not poison oak or stinging nettles) to insulate yourself from the cold ground.

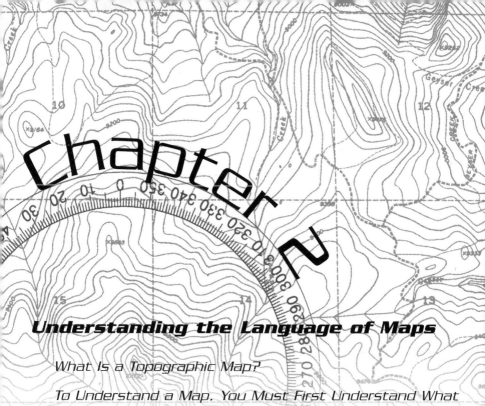

Chapter 2

Understanding the Language of Maps

Understanding the Language of Maps

What Is a Topographic Map?

A topographic map represents the three-dimensional lay of the land as viewed from directly overhead. It does this by using contour lines to show where hills, mountains, valleys, and canyons are located. A trained eye will see the three-dimensional images. Topographic maps are printed in color, with green depicting forested or vegetated areas and white indicating open terrain. Contour or elevation lines are printed in brown. Blue indicates water—either a lake, a river, or a stream. Black is used for man-made features such as trails, roads, and buildings. Man-made features on topographic maps other than privately produced ones such as those printed by Trails Illustrated, DeLorme, Earthwalk, and Harrison should be suspect; many U.S. Geological Survey (USGS) maps have not been revised in over twenty years. There are many other symbols used to depict such things as mines, ghost towns, marshes, swamps, waterfalls, and caves. The USGS does not print a key on each of its topographic maps, but rather on a separate sheet that may be obtained free from the USGS.

To Understand a Map, You Must First Understand What Information May Be Found Around Its Border or Margin

Around the edge of any map, you'll find numerous symbols, dashes, crosshatches, numbers, and words that offer essential meaning to the information printed on the map itself. The following list of numbered items corresponds with the sample USGS topographic map on pages 12-13 (Figure 2-1a-b).

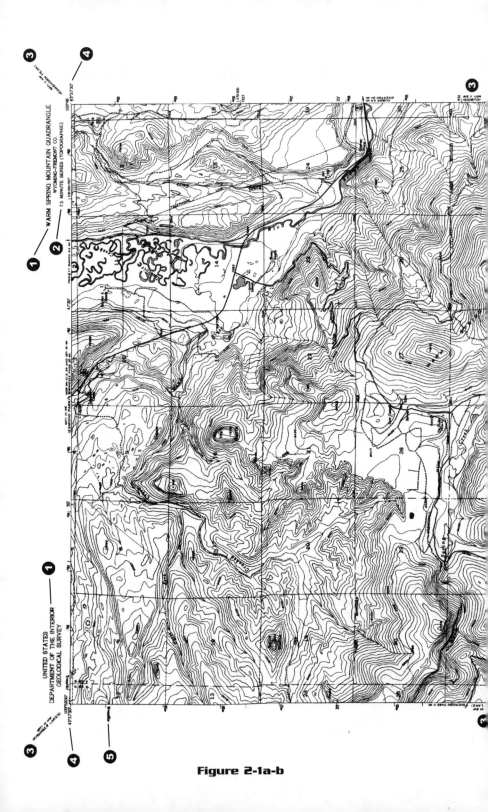

Figure 2-1a-b

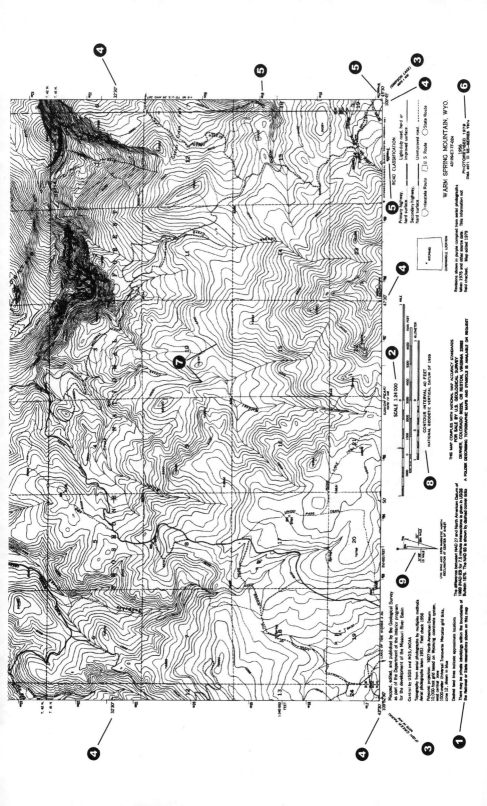

ROAD CLASSIFICATION

Primary highway,
hard surface _____

Light-duty road, hard or
improved surface _____

Secondary highway,
hard surface _____

Unimproved road ....

○ Interstate Route ○ U S Route ○ State Route

WARM SPRING MOUNTAIN, WYO.

43109-E7-TF-024

1956
PHOTOREVISED 1979
DMA 4471 III SE—SERIES V874

Revisions shown in purple compiled from aerial photographs
taken 1975 and other source data. This information not
field checked. Map edited 1979

RINGION PEAK
1030 IV NE

SCALE 1:24 000

CONTOUR INTERVAL 40 FEET
NATIONAL GEODETIC VERTICAL DATUM OF 1929

THIS MAP COMPLIES WITH NATIONAL MAP ACCURACY STANDARDS
FOR SALE BY U.S. GEOLOGICAL SURVEY
DENVER, COLORADO 80225, OR RESTON, VIRGINIA 22092
A FOLDER DESCRIBING TOPOGRAPHIC MAPS AND SYMBOLS IS AVAILABLE ON REQUEST

Mapped, edited, and published by the Geological Survey
as part of the Department of the Interior program
for the development of the Missouri River Basin

Control by USGS and NOS/NOAA

Topography from aerial photographs by multiple methods
Aerial photographs taken 1953. Field check 1956

Polyconic projection. 1927 North American Datum
10,000-foot grid based on Wyoming coordinate system,
west central zone
1000-meter Universal Transverse Mercator grid ticks,
zone 12, shown in blue

Dashed land lines indicate approximate locations

There may be private inholdings within the boundaries of
the National or State reservations shown on this map

The difference between NAD 27 and North American Datum
1983 (NAD 83) for 7.5 minute intersections is given in USGS
Bulletin 1875. The NAD 83 is shown by dashed corner ticks

UNDIVIDABLE LOCATION

WYOMING

UTM GRID AND 1979 MAGNETIC NORTH
DECLINATION AT CENTER OF SHEET

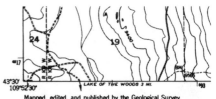

1 **Whose map is it and what area does it represent?** Somewhere on the map will be information regarding the map's creator or publisher and also the area the map covers. On USGS maps the publishing information appears in the lower left corner along the white border surrounding the map itself (Figure 2-2). The area the map covers is indicated in the upper right corner along the white border on a USGS map (Figure 2-3). The United States is divided into quadrants based on lines of latitude and longitude, and each quadrant most often carries the name of a significant geographic feature or municipality falling within its boundaries.

Mapped, edited, and published by the Geological Survey as part of the Department of the Interior program for the development of the Missouri River Basin

Control by USGS and NOS/NOAA

Topography from aerial photographs by multiplex methods Aerial photographs taken 1953. Field check 1956

Polyconic projection. 1927 North American Datum 10,000-foot grid based on Wyoming coordinate system, west central zone 1000-meter Universal Transverse Mercator grid ticks, zone 12, shown in blue

Dashed land lines indicate approximate locations

There may be private inholdings within the boundaries of the National or State reservations shown on this map

Figure 2-2

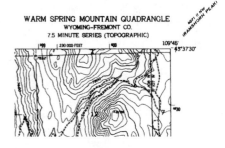

Figure 2-3

 What's the map's size (area of coverage) and scale? The USGS prints its maps in what are known as series (the 7.5-minute series, the 15-minute series). Although you can still find 15-minute series maps, the USGS prints primarily 7.5-minute series maps these days. To explain minutes, the earth is divided into 360 degrees of longitude (designating east and west) and 180 degrees of latitude (designating north and south). Each degree is divided into 60 units of measurement called minutes, and each minute is divided into 60 units of measurement called seconds. In navigational terms, minutes and seconds have absolutely nothing to do with time and everything to do with distance. A 7.5-minute series map represents an area of the earth's surface that is 7.5-minutes (⅛ degree) of longitude wide by 7.5 minutes (⅛ degree) of latitude high (Figure 2-4).

Typically, in a 7.5-minute map, the scale is 1:24,000, which means that every 1 unit of measurement on the map equals 24,000

units of the same measurement full sized. In a 1:24,000 scale map, 1 inch equals about 0.4 mile or nearly 2,000 feet. A 15-minute map is typically 1:62,500, which translates roughly to 1 inch equaling 1 mile. For navigational purposes, you will also find maps that are scaled 1:250,000, or 1 inch equaling 4 miles. This larger scale of map is useful for planning your trip, since it affords a big-picture, bird's-eye view of the terrain you'll be crossing. However, the map's scale is really too big to offer useful information when detailed map-in-the-hand field navigation is required (see appendix Figure A-5).

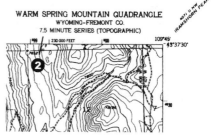

Figure 2-4

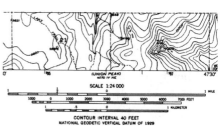

Figure 2-5

At the bottom of most maps is a bar scale that allows you to measure distances that correspond to feet, miles, and/or kilometers (Figure 2-5).

What maps adjoin the one you're looking at? Most maps print adjoining map information along their borders so that you can effectively link maps of the same series or scale and publisher. Typically, the names of corresponding and adjoining maps can be found printed at each corner, at each side, and at both the top and bottom of the map (Figure 2-6). Many maps also print

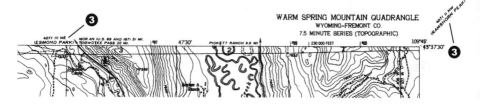

Figure 2-6

a silhouette picture of the region the map series covers, divided into equal quadrants; the map you're using will be the one that's shaded. This way you can visually see where the map fits in the entire region's mapping picture and how many adjoining maps might be required to navigate across it.

Find latitude and longitude. Degrees of latitude and longitude are indicated in the corners of most maps. Reading up from the bottom left or right corner of a map, changes in minutes and seconds of latitude (degrees are usually omitted unless the scale is so large that these, too, change between corners) are indicated by black ticks and/or fine black lines. Latitude in the Northern Hemisphere (north of the equator) increases as you move north and toward the top of the map. Reading left from the bottom right or top right corner of a map, changes in minutes and seconds of longitude (degrees are usually omitted unless the scale is so large that these, too, change between corners) are indicated by black ticks and/or fine black lines. Longitude in the Western Hemisphere (west of the Prime Meridian [International Date Line] running through Greenwich, England) increases as you go west up to 180 degrees. At 180 degrees you enter the Eastern Hemisphere, and longitude will begin to decrease (Figure 2-7).

On each map a pattern of squares or rectangles—called coordinate grids—is printed. These grids are made up of intersecting latitude and longitude lines and/or intersecting UTM easting and northing lines (UTM, or Universal Transverse Mercator, is explained below). Each location on a map corresponds to a unique set of coordinates that can be described by the corresponding latitude and longitude lines. Finding that location then becomes easy: Simply connect the indicated lines of latitude and longitude (or the UTM easting and northing lines) found marked along the map's borders (Figure 2-8).

Universal Transverse Mercator (UTM). Say what? UTM refers to the system grid that divides the entire world into sixty zones that are 6 degrees wide. The zones begin at east/west longitude 180 degrees and continue at 6-degree intervals.

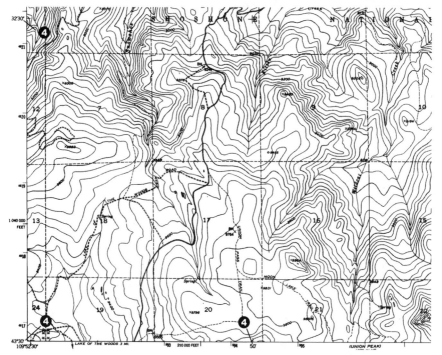

Figure 2-7

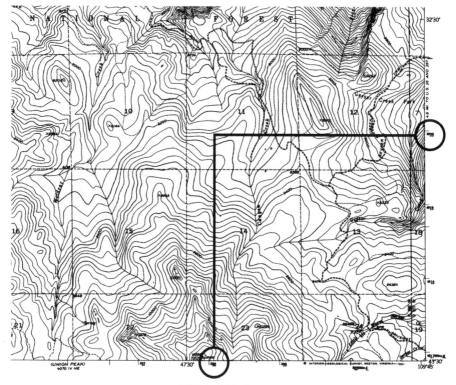

Figure 2-8

Each zone is then removed from the globe and flattened, losing its relationship to a sphere and introducing a certain amount of distortion. Since UTM projections distort the regions above 84 degrees north latitude and below 80 degrees south latitude far too much, these regions are not covered by maps using the UTM grid. The UTM grid is based upon the meter, and grid lines are always 1 kilometer (0.62 mile) apart, making it much easier to estimate distance on a map. UTM coordinates are printed on a map to indicate east–west and north-south positions (Figure 2-9). Numbers along the right side of a map are called northings (indicating the exact position north or south). Numbers along the top of the map are called eastings (indicating the exact position east or west). Making sense of the numbers is quick and easy:

❂ Increasing easting numbers indicate that you're heading east; decreasing numbers mean you're heading west. Increasing nor-

Figure 2-9

thing numbers indicate that you're heading north; decreasing numbers mean you're heading south.

✪ A reading of full UTM positions written along the right side of your map might go as follows: First mark (⁴35⁰⁰⁰m.N.), and then second mark (⁴36⁰⁰⁰m.N.). What does this mean? The larger numbers (35 and 36) indicate thousands of meters, and since 1,000 meters equals 1 kilometer, the two ticks are 1,000 meters or 1 kilometer apart. The last three numbers are printed smaller and indicate hundreds of meters. If the readings of the marks were (⁴35⁰⁰⁰m.N.) and then (⁴35⁵⁰⁰m.N.), this would indicate the ticks were 500 meters or 0.5 kilometer apart.

You need to understand UTM if you plan on working with Global Positioning System (GPS) or on using maps other than those printed by the USGS. The Bureau of Land Management (BLM) relies on the UTM system heavily. Many guidebooks and directions offered in descriptions give UTM bearings rather than latitude and longitude coordinates. For more information on UTM, see the appendix.

Revisions. Updates to USGS topographic maps are printed in the color purple with the date of the update appearing directly below the original printing date in the lower right corner (Figure 2-10; see also appendix Figure A-6). These updates include only photo-revised changes; they don't reflect actual field-checking. This is very useful information on USGS topographic maps, since the original surveys and data on which a map is based are often very old. No sense wasting valuable time and energy trying to find a trail that hasn't existed in decades even though it appears on this fifty-year-old map!

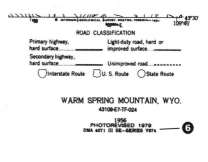

Figure 2-10

Contour lines.

7 Contour lines are the brown squiggly lines on a topographic map that seem rather confusing at first glance but are really very precise representations of geography in the area the map covers. Each contour line is comprised of an often irregular closed loop that connects points of equal elevation. The line with a darker shade of brown, typically

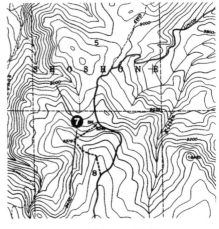

Figure 2-11

every fifth line, is called an index contour and usually has the elevation printed on it (Figure 2-11).

8 **Contour interval.** To correctly read the severity of the terrain's ups and downs, you must know the contour interval, printed at the bottom of the map. The contour interval indicates the elevation change between adjacent contour lines (Figure 2-12).

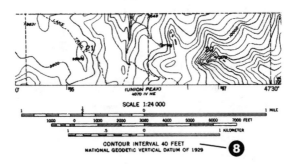

Figure 2-12

9 **Declination.** At the bottom of each map is a declination illustration. The diagram shows three variations in direction: the geographic North Pole, indicated by a line with star on the top of it and pointing toward the top of the globe; the magnetic north pole, indicated by a line with MN on the top of it and pointing toward the magnetic north pole (the area a magnetic needle on a compass points to); and the grid north pole, a line with GN on the top of it. Grid north pole refers to the Universal Transverse Mercator grid designed by cartographers to reduce the distortion created by transferring the earth's curvature to a flat map surface. For the purposes of declination, only geographic north and magnetic north and the degree of difference east or west between the two are of importance. The degrees of declination are printed alongside the illustration. You can determine if the indicated declination is east or west by which side of the geographic North Pole line the magnetic north pole line is printed. If it's printed to the right, it's an east declination; to the left, a west declination. This is important because it will indicate whether you add or subtract degrees to correct your compass reading (Figure 2-13; see also appendix Figure A-6).

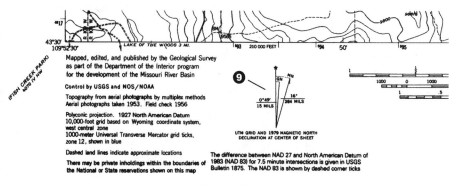

Figure 2-13

Reading the Lay of the Land from the Story Your Map Tells

How Do You Read Contour Lines?

In general:

❂ Widely spaced contour lines indicate a gradual slope.

❂ The more packed together the contour lines are, the steeper and more severe the terrain. Closely spaced contours may mean a cliff.

✪ Contours that roughly form circles getting smaller in size with each gain in elevation indicate hills or mountain peaks. A summit is often marked with an X; the number next to it indicates the exact elevation of that peak.

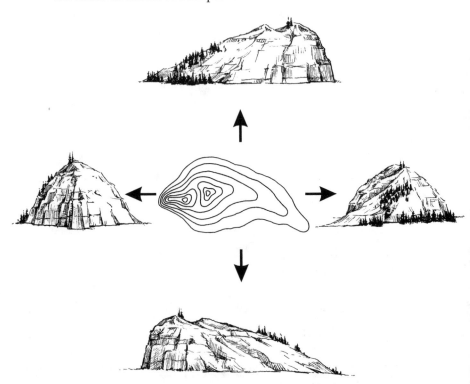

Figure 2-14 Learning to visualize what a map image of a 3-D object looks like—such as this rocky outcropping—is a valuable skill.

✪ Contour lines that bend into V shapes (the Vs may look more like Us if the terrain is sloping very gently) represent either a canyon or a sloping ridge. If the Vs are pointing uphill, toward a point of higher elevation, then the Vs are forming a canyon. If the Vs are pointing downhill, toward a point of lower elevation then they form a ridge. It stands to reason that a stream in a V would indicate that the V is a canyon pointing toward higher elevations (Figure 2-15).

✪ V-shaped valleys on a map are typically steep in nature and more difficult to navigate. If the V shape is extremely pronounced, expect the sidewalls of the canyon to be steep and almost impossible to scramble up or down. Once you're on the canyon floor, you're probably there to stay until you exit either up- or downstream. U-shaped valleys, on the other hand, are far gentler and, consequently, easier to navigate (Figure 2-15).

How Significant Is the Map's Contour Interval?

Aside from telling you how steep the terrain is, the interval offers another bit of critical information. Consider a map with a contour interval of 40 feet. This means the cartographer drew a contour line on the map for every 40 feet of elevation change up or down. What this also means is that a rather large (to you, when standing in front of it) 30-foot rocky outcropping, or

Figure 2-15

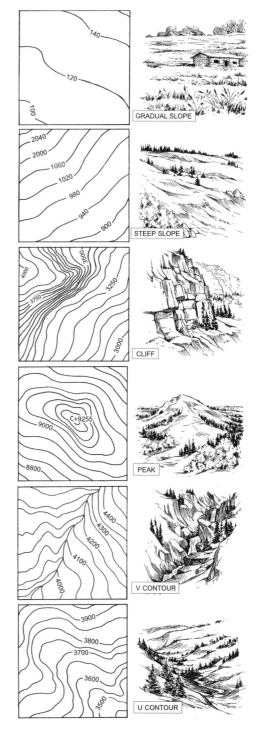

35-foot cliff, or 25-foot-deep wash won't show up on the map if it falls between the appointed contour interval markings (Figure 2-16).

Just because the map doesn't show a geographic feature doesn't mean the feature doesn't exist. I've seen countless navigational errors made—a few of them made by me—because of a geographic feature that isn't on the map. This mystical feature, when viewed within the context of "this map tells the entire truth so that feature must be this feature on the map (even though it isn't)" and "it must be right here which means we are right there (even though we aren't)," can really ruin your day—*oops*! Keep in mind that if you're standing directly in front of the 35-foot rocky hill that isn't on the map, it will also be blocking from your view features that do exist on the map, making orienting yourself that much more difficult unless you're able to determine the interference and move to a better vantage point.

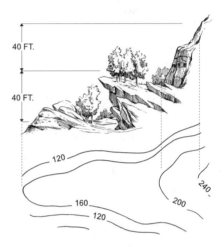

Figure 2-16

Your use of any map and its ability to be able to help you find your way are only as good as your ability to interpret the size and shape of the geography and relate it to the map that's interpreting it. You must also remember that a map is only one part of the navigational puzzle, and you need all the pieces in order to find your way with consistent accuracy.

Using Your Map's Scale to Estimate Trip Distance

Estimating the distance of your trip is useful if you wish to ensure that you can actually complete your trip in a safe period of time. Of course, distance is only one part of the equation. You must also factor in elevation loss and gain, which will make your route longer and increase the effort required to travel it, in effect adding to the time needed to get from point A to point B.

Although the bar scale printed at the bottom of your map is straight, I have yet to find many naturally occurring straight lines in the great outdoors. Trails, waterways, and canyons meander from here to there, making it that much more difficult—though not impossible—to estimate how far, how long.

There are a number of measuring wheels on the market, some of which actually work quite well. Still, they aren't perfect; they represent more bulk to carry into the field, and they must be used very carefully on an absolutely flat surface. Many compasses also include map measuring scales on their baseplates, but again, these require a certain amount of calculation and offer only very rough "straight point-A-to-point-B" measuring (Figure 2-17). My pre-

ferred method of measuring distance relies on narrow-gauge electrical wire, colored white or red. Electrical wire—the kind used in model building—is very flexible, holds its shape, doesn't stretch, and can be marked with an indelible ink marker. Cut a 12-inch section of the wire and then mark 0.25-mile and 1-mile increments on it with a fine-tipped indelible black ink marker. I have found that using dots for the 0.25-mile marks and a complete band around the wire for the 1-mile marks works best. Be sure to meticulously match your marks to those on the map's bar scale (Figure 2-18).

Place one end of the wire at your starting point and then gradually bend and contour the wire to match the twists and

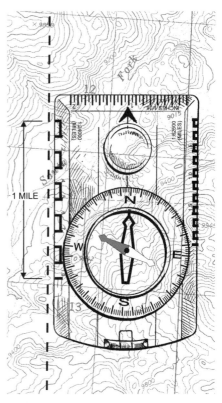

Figure 2-17

bends of your trail or
route of travel (Figure
2-19). Once the bend-
ing and contouring is
finished, you can
count up the miles
and determine just
how far your planned
route is, how far it
might be to your esti-
mated rest points,
and how far it is to

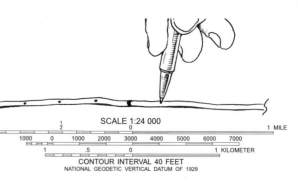

Figure 2-18

points of scenic interest, water, and other landmarks. With the
wire in place, you can also assemble a fairly decent trail profile that
affords a very reality-based image of how steep the ups and downs
really are.

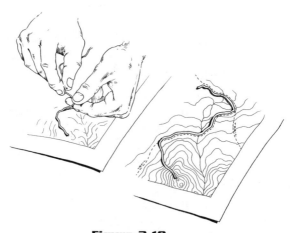

Figure 2-19

Creating a Trail Profile

One mile as the crow flies is not necessarily representative of 1 mile
as the trail climbs. For one thing, although the horizontal distance
may be 1 mile, the hypotenuse (oh gawd . . . it's math. Hypotenuse:
the side of a right-angled triangle opposite the right angle) is
longer if the vertical distance or elevation gained is greater. Huh?!

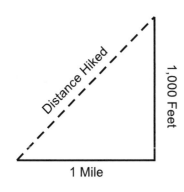

Figure 2-20 Actual distance hiked is more than 1 mile.

Okay, check out the diagram (Figure 2-20). It's also quite difficult to estimate just how steep the route you're going to travel might be. This is where a good trail profile comes in.

On my computer-generated maps, all I do is press a button and, presto, a neat trail profile appears on the screen. In most instances, though, the area I'm traveling in isn't covered by a computerized map. Soooo, I must resort to manual modes of estimation—which is why you left the wire in place after estimating your travel distance. Grab a sheet of paper and draw a straight vertical line up the left side. Beginning at the bottom of the vertical line, draw a horizontal line at a 90-degree angle and across the page to the right. Place marks on the vertical line that represent the contour interval found on the map, working upward from the point of lowest elevation on your route of travel to the highest. Along the horizontal line, place marks every 0.25-mile, matching the bar scale on the map. Using a pencil, draw horizontal lines for every contour line, and draw vertical lines for every 0.5-mile (every 0.25-mile gets to be a bit much, and it's easy enough to estimate the middle of a short line to mark 0.25-mile increments if needed).

With pencil in hand, begin visually traveling along the wire following your route of travel, first marking the point of elevation at mile 0 and then points of elevation for every 0.25 mile of distance traveled. Once you have all the points marked on your paper graph, connect the dots and, presto, you'll have a very enlightening visual presentation that should demonstrate just what you're in for (Figure 2-21).

Finding Yourself on the Map

A map is of absolutely no use to you unless you can place yourself somewhere on it with accuracy and then be able to determine where you might want to head or where you've come from. To do this, you must first orient the map so that it represents a one-dimensional image that comes as close as possible to paralleling the three-dimensional world you're standing in; the map and the real world become one in your mind (Figure 2-22).

How Do You Orient a Map Without a Compass?

The easiest way to orient a map is by using readily identifiable landmarks. This is easier said than done, however, if you've no idea where you are right now. First, you have to determine roughly where you are on the map. Again, landmarks offer the best clues. If you can easily and assuredly identify a nearby landmark (such as a readily identifiable peak, a well-known and easily recognized river, a fire tower, a major roadway or trail, or a sign) that's unique enough to have a map symbol or designation, then you're home free. Of course, there is the possibility that while you may be able to recognize a road, trail, river, or shoreline, you may not be able to tell where you are on it. No matter. Roads, trails, fence lines, power lines, rivers, shorelines, and similar landmarks fall under the wonderful category

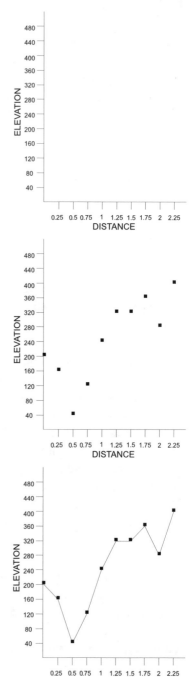

Figure 2-21

of baselines. A baseline is an easily identified feature of length that stands out and is clearly marked on the map. Once you find yourself on a baseline, you simply walk up and down it until you come to another identifiable point. It could even be another baseline intersecting the one you're on. You can now place yourself most assuredly on the

Figure 2-22

map. If you think about it, whenever you offer up directions, you probably give intersecting baselines as a means of helping others. "My house is right near the intersection of Mountain Avenue [one baseline] and River Boulevard [another baseline] (Figure 2-23)."

Once you know your exact position on the map, it becomes a fairly simple matter to spin the map until other points of reference on it line up with the same points of reference found before you on the surrounding landscape. Good navigators keep their maps in constant orientation to the surrounding landscape as they travel. Yes, this means that sometimes the maps are upside down, which

makes reading map symbols and names a bit of a creative exercise, but this is far better than carrying the map right-side up and trying to mentally rotate the landscape or map to compensate. The latter method is pure idiocy, in my opinion. Learning to read upside down is far easier and had less potential for navigational disaster.

Figure 2-23

What if You Can Orient the Map Successfully, but Still Don't Know Exactly Where You Are?

Sometimes the surrounding landscape is so big or unique that it's an easy task to orient the map. This is often the case in a desert environment when distant landmarks are readily visible and identifiable, making map orientation a relatively simple process. But how do you know just where you are in the vast expanse of unrecognizable bumps and sandy or rocky undulations? Easy. Pick out three identifiable landmarks, preferably one ahead to the right, one ahead to the left, and one off to the side. With the map oriented and lying flat on the ground, lay a straightedge on the map with the center of the straightedge on the map landmark (Figure 2-24). Now spin the straightedge until one end points straight at the actual landmark. Draw a line across the map. Repeat the process with the other two points. The intersection of these three lines will indicate your rough position, accurate to within 0.25 mile if you were careful (Figure 2-25). Always double-check your efforts, and then carefully compare what the map says is your approximate position with your surrounding landscape to be sure the visual information matches.

Caring for Your Map

How Do You Waterproof a Map?

There's no fun in trying to navigate while clinging to a soggy map in a downpour. Right before your eyes, the route home begins to turn into a greenish brown papier mâché clump. Your only hope at this point is that your memory of the route doesn't wash out like the map did.

Making a see-though, waterproof cover for your map is an easy way to prevent soggy-map syndrome. All you need is a large, freezer-weight Ziploc bag and a few sections of sturdy, waterproof tape like duct or packing tape.

Simply cut the tape into a strip long enough to completely adhere to one edge of the bag from top to bottom. Press one half of the tape, lengthwise, onto the side edge of the bag, leaving the other half of the tape hanging over the edge. Now flip the bag over, and fold the tape down on itself and the other side of the bag.

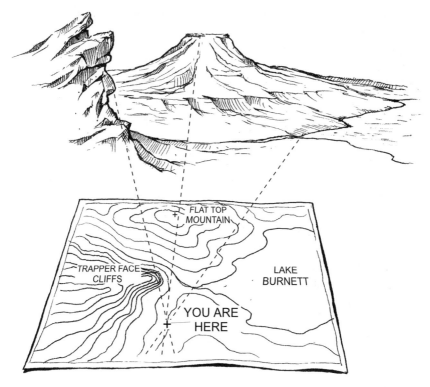

Figure 2-24, 25

Repeat each step twice more, once for the bottom and once for the remaining side. You now have a wonderful waterproof map container that's reinforced on three edges.

There are several other ways to waterproof a map:

⚙ Covering a map with clear contact paper makes it waterproof but very stiff, and you can no longer write on it with a pencil. You can, however, use an indelible ink marker to highlight your route or make notes. When done, clean up the marks with a gauze pad soaked in rubbing alcohol.

⚙ Paint on a product called Stormproof or other map waterproofing treatments by Aquaseal or Nikwax—available at most map and outdoor specialty stores. These clear chemical coatings render the map waterproof, yet it remains flexible and can be written on.

✪ A coating of Thompson Water Seal or another brick and masonry sealant will make a map water repellent but not water-proof.

Folding a Map

Map folding is an acquired skill. Add a blowing wind, a little rain, and a sprinkling of fatigue and what you get is an irresistible desire to jam or crumple your trail map into the nearest pocket and forget the idea of folding.

Believe it or not, there is a better way—a map-folding technique that results in a very easy-to-use accordion-style configuration. It's taught to British Boy Scouts; my cousin from England can fold a map like this in his sleep.

This method allows you to look at any portion of the map without having to fully open it, which is ideal in windy or wet weather. Further, the accordion configuration collapses to pocket size with ease. Once you've established the creases, any map will fold up and down almost without effort.

Step 1 Lay the map flat, printed-side up. Fold it in half vertically, with the face inside the first fold to establish the first crease. Make this and every subsequent crease clean and sharp.

Step 2 Working with only the right half of the map, fold the right side in half toward the center, resulting in one quarter-fold.

Step 3 Fold the outside quarter-fold back to the edge, producing an eighth-fold. Use this fold as a guide and fold the other quarter the same way—trust me, it's easier than it sounds.

Step 4 Half the map should now have four accordion-style folds.

Step 5 Repeat steps 2 and 3 on the map's other half so that you end up with a full accordion of eight folds in a long rulerlike shape.

Step 6 Finally, fold the map in the shape of a Z so it's in thirds. Voilà! Now you can look at any section without having to completely unfold the map, and it will snap into place almost by itself (Figure 2-26).

A Map Has Its Limitations

Earlier I spoke of one map limitation: Some features don't show up because their elevation falls between the contour intervals. But there are other limitations to a topographic map, too—the most obvious being the man-made features shown. These were accurate only at the time the map was surveyed. New buildings may have been built and old ones torn down, new roads constructed and old ones left to deteriorate, new trails built and old ones left to return to the land. Never, ever fall into the trap of resting your navigation-

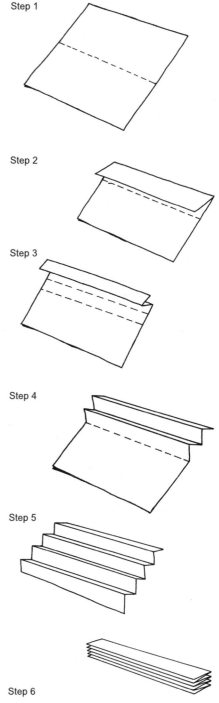

Step 1

Step 2

Step 3

Step 4

Step 5

Step 6

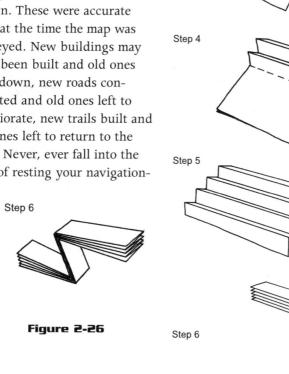

Step 6

Figure 2-26

al hopes on man-made features.

Consider, too, that because the map can provide only so much information, a complete picture of how easy or difficult the terrain is to negotiate may not be evident until you're actually attempting to navigate your way through it. A number of years back, while mountaineering in the Wind River Range of Wyoming, my partner and I made our way to what appeared on the map to be a slope of such extreme steepness that we would need ropes to scale it. Upon arriving at the base, we found the slope to be steep but covered with a layer of stable scree bisected by a wildlife trail snaking its way to the top. We followed it without difficulty.

Many are the times that I have encountered boulder fields too massive and unstable to cross safely, even though the map indicated a relatively gentle contour interval. Deep sand that sucked the life out of my legs, pea-sized gravel that made walking an adventure similar to wandering across a concrete floor covered with ball bearings, and deep muck under a layer of grass where a wonderful open meadow was supposed to exist are just a few of the adventures I've experienced—all reminders that what the map says and what reality dictates exist often on two completely different planes.

Finally, even with the best map, complete with the most assuredly accurate information, it's virtually impossible to navigate regions that are heavily treed, or shrouded in darkness, or blessed with feature after similar feature (as in deserts, prairies, and snowfields). For this kind of navigational situation, you must add a compass.

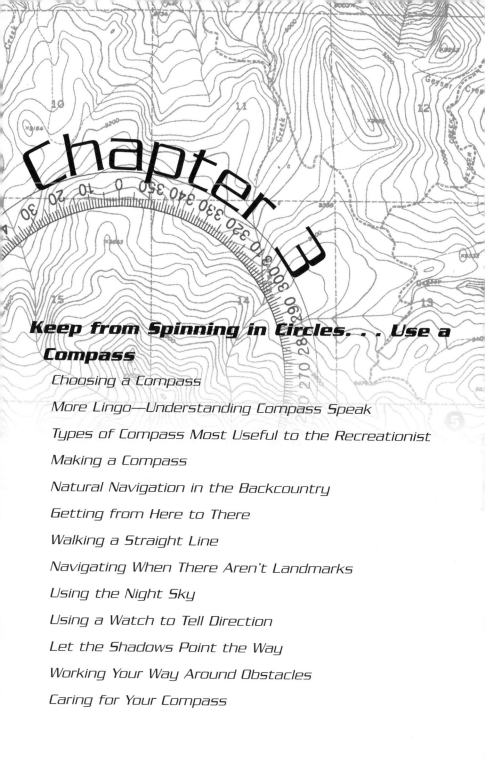

chapter 3

Keep from Spinning in Circles. . . Use a Compass

Keep from Spinning in Circles . . . Use a Compass

Choosing a Compass

What's the Best Compass for You?

That depends on the intended end use and how much money you wish to spend. The four most popular brands of compass are Brunton, Nexus, Silva, and Suunto. Each company offers numerous models, each with a specific purpose and different features but all with essentially the same role—to help you determine direction, plot a course, and stay on it.

At a minimum a compass should feature a rotating bezel with a 360-degree dial in 2-degree graduations, a clear baseplate with inch and millimeter scales, a direction-of-travel arrow engraved into the baseplate, and a rotating magnetic needle mounted in a clear capsule filled with liquid to reduce shake and movement. Orienting lines should also be engraved or printed on the bottom of the rotating capsule. A basic compass costs around $10. Additional features such as a sighting mirror, a built-in adjustable declination, a clinometer, and a magnifying glass will add to this cost. For maximum accuracy you want a compass with a sighting mirror (often referred to as a prismatic-type compass), because this allows you to hold the compass at eye level, line up the landmark in the notched sight at the top of the mirror, and read the compass bearing using the mirror. With a mirror, the accuracy level of sighting improves from approximately 5 degrees of error, using a simple baseplate compass, to about 2 degrees of error or better.

Do You Really Need a Compass That Adjusts for Declination?

The difference between the true north shown on a topographic map and the magnetic north indicated by a compass needle is known as declination. Declination is either west or east, depending on which side of true or geographic north the needle points. On USGS topographic maps declination is indicated by arrows printed on the bottom margin. The arrow with a star above it indicates true or geographic north. The shorter arrow with an MN above it indicates magnetic north. If the MN arrow is on the left side of the true–north arrow, your declination is west; *add* the indicated degree amount to correct your bearing. If the MN arrow is on the right side of the true-north arrow, your declination is east, and you will *subtract* the indicated degree amount to correct your bearing. While it's easy enough to do this manually (depending on your math proficiency), a compass that features a built-in declination adjustment allows you to turn a screw or adjust the housing so the compass will read true. You just have to remember that each time declination changes, often from map to map, you must manually adjust your compass to the new setting. (See Figure A-3, World Variation Chart).

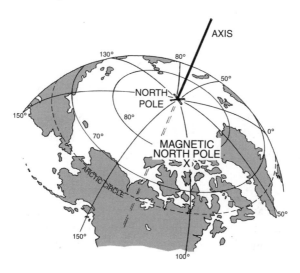

Figure 3-1

What the Heck is a Clinometer and Why Would You Need One?

A clinometer is used to measure vertical angles, the slope of hills, or other objects and is especially useful if you are planning to do any serious snowshoeing, backcountry skiing, or winter mountaineering where avalanches might become a concern. With a clinometer, you will be able to estimate accurately the steepness of terrain and determine the degree of risk of avalanche danger.

One other use is to measure the height or width of an object. The principle reaches back into ninth grade geometry class and something called a "right triangle." Remember? One of the angles of a right triangle has to be ninety degrees. What this means is that you can stand at the base of a cliff of which you wish to measure the height and walk away from the cliff until the top of the cliff is equal to forty-five degrees. The distance you walked away plus your height is also the height of the cliff—give or take a few feet. Why? Brace yourself, because I'm going to toss some math concepts your way again. When there is one 45-degree angle on a "right triangle," the third angle must be 45 degrees also. In this case your right triangle is actually an isosceles triangle, meaning that the triangle not only has the two 45 degree angles and one 90 degree angle, but also has two sides the same length. In this example the distance you walked from the cliff plus your height and the measured height of the cliff are the same.

45°

Your height

Distance

Figure 3-2

Other than winter use and measuring height, however, a clinometer doesn't offer much for the recreational user other than a way to determine slope angle and the ability to say, "We hiked up a 45-degree slope . . . wahooo!"

Can You Use a Compass Anywhere in the World?

Yes, you can. True, there are "global compasses" sold to those who are traveling into the far reaches of the Northern or Southern Hemisphere, but frankly, they're a bit of overkill and often far more fragile than other models.

Essentially, what happens to a compass needle as you move farther north is that magnetic forces pull harder on its north end, tilting it toward the bottom of the compass housing. In the south, magnetic forces pull harder on the south end of the needle, tilting it toward the bottom of the compass. What this means is that you have to tilt your compass to compensate for the needle tilt and allow the needle to float freely enough for you to take a sighting. This can present a bit of a challenge when you're trying to sight. However, unless you're surveying, the results will still be plenty accurate.

If you do want as much accuracy as possible, you can go several routes. First, you can purchase a global compass. These compasses have their needles built on a kind of double-hinge system, which increases the tilt tolerance of the needle. The drawback is that they're nowhere near as durable. I've broken one simply by tossing it into and out of a pack. (You can always purchase a compass specifically balanced for the hemisphere you will be traveling. See Figure A-4, World Balancing Chart).

Your other alternative is to use an electronic compass . . . read on.

How Good are Electronic Compasses?

Electronic compasses are very good. Both the handheld variety, such as the Brunton Outback, and the wrist-top variety, such as the Suunto Vector, offer global functionality. The Outback has gimbal-mounted sensors inside, which keep the sensor level (essential for accurate readings) even if the unit is tipped up to 20 degrees from level. The Suunto requires the use of a level bubble, but even this is a major improvement over electronic watches that have no such feature. If an electronic compass has no level or is not gimbal-mounted, your bearings can be off by as much as 15 degrees. Both compasses can be adjusted electronically for magnetic declination.

With handheld electronic compasses, the benefits mount. Since the compass is, basically, a computer, it allows for memory entry.

You can store bearings and back them, making it feasible to pre-plan a trip and preprogram the route. You can also enter bearings as you travel, making it easier to retrace your steps.

Of course, don't for a minute think that electronics provide navigational nirvana. The accuracy of a digital compass generally isn't as good as an equivalently priced analog or standard compass. If your electronic compass loses power for any reason, you can lose all your data, leaving you feeling a little lost. If you experience interference from a magnetic field, such as a belt buckle, building, or radio tower, you won't know it; with a standard compass, on the other hand, it's easy to see any pull in one direction or another. And finally, most digital compasses don't feature printed-on scales, making it really difficult to measure distances.

More Lingo—Understanding Compass Speak

Azimuth Ring (Housing): This is the circular housing on the compass; it has textured edges and is often filled with liquid. It rotates within the compass base for taking or setting bearings. Degree markings, from 0 to 360, are typically etched into its surface to make up the azimuth ring or graduated dial.

Gun-Type Sights: Most often found on prismatic (sighting) compasses, these are used like the sights on a gun for sighting and taking bearings with maximum accuracy.

Index Line: The mark on the front of the sight or compass baseplate where you will read the indicated bearing.

Line of Travel or Direction of Travel: A line or arrow engraved on the baseplate of your compass that points you in the direction you need to go to get to your desired destination.

Liquid Damping: This allows the needle to come to a rest rapidly and helps hold it steady, allowing for faster and more accurate readings. Compasses that don't have liquid damping leave you waiting for what seems like a lifetime for the needle to stop spinning—and then leaves you squinting to determine where the bouncy needle is actually pointing. Better compasses use a kerosene-based fluid or some other additive to ensure that the liquid doesn't

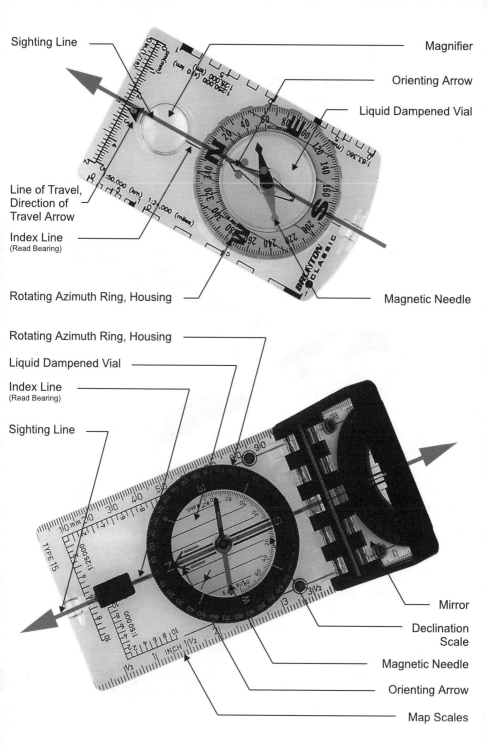

Sighting Line

Magnifier

Orienting Arrow

Liquid Dampened Vial

Line of Travel, Direction of Travel Arrow

Index Line
(Read Bearing)

Rotating Azimuth Ring, Housing

Magnetic Needle

Rotating Azimuth Ring, Housing

Liquid Dampened Vial

Index Line
(Read Bearing)

Sighting Line

Mirror

Declination Scale

Magnetic Needle

Orienting Arrow

Map Scales

Figure 3-3

freeze or boil from -40 degrees to 120 degrees.

Magnifier: The sole purpose of this feature is to assist you in reading the often extremely small print on a map.

Mirror: Incorporated into a hard-case lid that folds down over the top of the compass housing, the mirror is used to make prismatic in-line sightings—the most accurate method of using a handheld compass. A prismatic compass can be held at eye level so you can sight the distant object and the compass face at the same time.

Orienting Arrow: This is the outlined arrow engraved into the base of your compass housing and often lined with red paint. It exactly outlines the outside of the magnetic needle. By centering or "boxing" the magnetic needle within the orienting arrow's outline, both pointing in the same direction (unless you're back-sighting), you can determine your bearing or direction of travel.

Protractor: Some models have this feature, which allows you to more easily plot a bearing on a map.

Sighting Line: This is the line you sight along on a handheld compass to take a bearing.

Types of Compass Most Useful to the Recreationist

While each company's line-up of compasses has its own particular idiosyncrasies relative to features, the following descriptions are fairly accurate across the board.

Simple (Starter-Type) Compass: These usually feature 5-degree increments, orienting arrows, and simple map measuring scales.

Basic Baseplate Compasses: Usually feature 2-degree increments, orienting arrows, more detailed measuring scales, and sometimes lanyards (Figure 3-4).

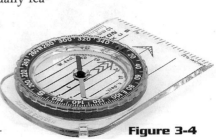

Basic Baseplate Compasses with Declination Scale: Usually feature 2-degree increments, orienting arrows, more detailed measuring

Figure 3-4

scales, lanyards, and built-in
adjustable declination correction
scales. They sometimes include
magnifying glasses and nighttime glow-in-the-dark markings
(Figures 3-5 and 3-6).

Figure 3-5

**Mirrored/Sighting
Compasses:** Usually feature 2-
degree increments, orienting
arrows, more detailed measuring
scales, lanyards, fixed or
adjustable declination correction
scales, and sighting mirrors.
They sometimes include magnifying glasses and nighttime
glow-in-the-dark markings. They
offer accuracy of scale of up to 1
degree when you're sighting
(Figure 3-7).

Figure 3-6

**Orienteering or
Competition Compasses:**
Usually feature 2-degree increments, orienting arrows, very
detailed measuring scales (sometimes interchangeable),
adjustable declination correction
scales, antislip rubber pads, magnifying glasses, heavier needles
and special damping fluid for
quicker readings, map templates
for marking controls, and lanyards. They sometimes include
clinometers (Figure 3-8).

Figure 3-7

Sighting Compasses: Usually
feature 1-degree increments,
optics, and accuracy of scale to ½
degree. Sometimes electronic,

Figure 3-8

Figure 3-9

these units are primarily intended for professional use when accuracy to the nth degree is critical. The Brunton Pocket Transit and Pro-Line Outdoorsman Series fall into this category. While recreationists can and do use such compasses, they don't have a baseplate and consequently are not as easily used with a map.

This type of compass is best suited for those times when route finding will be done by compass alone (Figure 3-9).

Other Compass Types

The compasses listed above are, in my opinion, the best choices for the recreational user, but there are a couple of others you might encounter.

Fixed Dial Compasses: These are affixed to watchbands, knife handles, or zipper pull-tabs—and are also sold as very simple handheld compasses.

Figure 3-10

They feature molded plastic cases, typically with 5-degree increments engraved in. There's no baseplate and no way to adjust for declination short of mathematical calculation. These compasses are basically useless for anything more than simple compass-only route-finding applications (Figure 3-10).

Military-Style Lensatic Compasses: Since these are sold through military surplus stores and numerous discount warehouses, they're popular. They come with a forward and rear sight and a lens with a line in it used to read and establish a bearing. Since they have no baseplate, it's very difficult to use them effectively with a map. Their claim of improved accuracy over a mirrored sighting compass is debatable at best (Figure 3-11).

Figure 3-11

Compass Type	Hiking/ Fishing	Off-Trail Mountaineering	General/ Scouts	Orientering/ Competition	Professional
Simple (starter type)	yes	no	yes	no	no
Basic Baseplate	yes	no	yes	yes	no
Basic Baseplate with declination scale	yes	yes	yes	yes	no
Mirror/Sighting	yes	yes	yes	yes	yes
Orienteering	no	no	no	yes	no
Sighting	no	yes	no	no	yes
Electronic	yes	yes	yes	no	no

Electronic: Provides magnetic sensing and memory-saving functions. Accuracy can be as good as 5 degrees but as poor as 20 degrees if you don't hold the compass level. Not recommended as your primary compass (Figure 3-12).

Figure 3-12

Compass without Needles: Brunton has created a new type of compass that removes the needle and instead creates a proprietary circle-over-circle matching system that offers 1-degree sighting accuracy. Matching the dots instead of the traditional boxing of a needle removes one commonly made element of error in reading a compass (Figure 3-13).

Making a Compass

Nothing will help you understand how a compass works like making one. Learning the principles will also be useful if you ever find yourself having to rig a compass.

Figure 3-13

Schoolchildren the world over have for decades been making compasses out of a needle and cork, and the following tutorial is right out of almost any fifth-grade science text.

Fill a nonmetal container such as a cup or a bowl with water. Take a wine bottle cork and slice a ½-inch-thick section off the narrower end. Suspend a steel needle in the water by sticking it through the top third of the cork so that, when the cork is placed in the water, the unit floats with the needle remaining clear of the water. Then stroke the sharp end of the needle repeatedly and in the same direction with a magnet. The magnetized end of the needle will now point toward magnetic north. You may have to remagnetize the needle every so often.

So how does this help you in a survival situation? Keep in mind that every radio, including those found in vehicles, uses a magnet as part of its speaker. Don't have a cork? So find a twig or a wooden matchstick or anything else that will float freely. No nonmetallic container for water, or no water at all? Don't fret. Hang the needle from a very fine thread, making sure that it isn't twisted. No needle? Anything metal will suffice, including small nails, pins, or the edge of a razor blade—it just has to be made of metal that can be magnetized. Not sure whether the metal you're using can be magnetized? Try picking it up with the magnet. If the magnet attracts the metal, you can magnetize it.

For those of you who are really in an experimental mood, you can magnetize a needle or nail or other strip of metal with nothing more than insulated copper wire (found inside most radios or other electrical gear) and a battery that generates at least six volts of charge. Wrap a length of insulated copper wire around the metal approximately twenty-five to forty times. Connect each end of the wire to your battery's terminals. It takes about twenty-five to forty-five minutes to effectively magnetize the metal. When the time is up, suspend the needle or nail or other metal of choice (as indicated in the paragraphs above). The end that points toward north will be the end that was nearest the negative (-) terminal on the battery— N for negative or north. My science teacher loved this experiment, sometimes, I think, a little too much!

Natural Navigation in the Backcountry

Staying on course when you're stepping a lively beat down a trail is relatively simple—just stay alert, follow the trail, and read the signs. Off trail, especially on snowfields, ice floes and desert sands, route finding is an entirely different beast. A compass is an invaluable aid, but so is an observant eye. When miles and miles of trackless terrain exists, taking note of the prevailing wind direction and the resulting textures it leaves on the land offers essential information. On tundra and sea ice in the Arctic, systematic drift patterns in the snow—sastrugi—offer a valuable directional clue. Use a compass to check on the directional formations of these patterns, and then remember them. The same is true of sand drifts in desert environments. Taking note of these physical directional clues becomes invaluable if a sandstorm or snowstorm whips up that limits your visibility and impairs the taking of distant compass bearing points. In such conditions you can use sand drifts or sastrugi underfoot to help you stay generally on track rather than wandering endlessly in circles.

Other natural clues can also aid in staying your course. On the coast of the ocean, for example, or any other large body of water, prevailing winds typically blow offshore during the morning hours and back onshore as the sun sets—a result of the heating and then cooling of the earth inland.

Forget the old adage, Moss grows on the north side of a tree. Moss grows wherever it's cool and damp. Most frequently this is on either the north or the south side of a tree—the sides that receive the least amount of sun throughout a day.

Getting from Here to There

One of the most valuable things about a compass is that it will assist you in getting from point A to point B, even if you lose sight of B along the way. How? Begin by taking a bearing. Say what? Take a bearing, which means holding your compass level and pointing its direction-of-travel arrow directly at the landmark you want to head toward. Then, with the arrow pointed at the landmark (point B), turn the housing until the orienting arrow points the same way and boxes (surrounds) the floating magnetic needle.

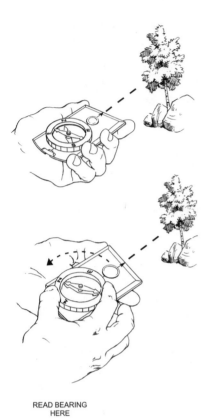

Now read the degree of heading indicated on the housing and adjacent to the index point. This degree reading is your heading. As you hike off from point A and descend into the woods, all you have to do is keep walking in the direction indicated by the direction-of-travel arrow when the magnetic needle is boxed by the orienting arrow and the housing is turned to place the established degree bearing at the index point. Simple? Yes and no. Even if you walk for miles in the direction indicated by your compass, you can still end up vastly off course. How? By drifting right or left as you walk, a very common mistake.

Walking a Straight Line

You can correct for drift and ensure that you always walk a straight line from point A to point B by navigating point to point along the way. Once you have established your bearing, sight along the direction-of-travel arrow to establish an intermediate landmark—one you won't lose sight of along the way—and hike directly toward it. Once you're there, sight along your compass again, being sure it's set to the correct heading, and establish another landmark to hike toward. In this way you'll hike point to point all the way

READ BEARING
HERE

Figure 3-14

to point B in as straight a line as possible.

If you ever have any doubt as to your chosen route of travel (it's possible to arrive at your intermediate landmark and not know if the boulder or tree or peak where you are is the correct landmark if another, similar-looking landmark exists nearby), take a back-sighting. You do this by turning around and facing your point of origin (assuming it's still visible) or your last established and still-identifiable landmark. Point your direction-of-travel arrow directly at the landmark and center (box) the magnetic needle with the orienting arrow—only this time the needle and the arrow will point in opposite directions. If you cannot center (box) the needle, don't move the housing. Instead, move to the right or left until you can center (box) the needle by repointing the arrow. Now you're back on course.

Learning to establish a back bearing is very useful if you decide to cut your trip short for any reason and head back to point A, your point of origin. Once the needle is boxed, rotate the housing until both the magnetic needle and the orienting arrow are pointing the same way. Now read the new degree bearing at the index point. You can achieve the same effect by performing a little math as well. If your original heading was 180 degrees (due south), then a back bearing or return trip would be 360 degrees (due north). The formula for this is: For bearings greater than 180, subtract 180 degrees to arrive at the correct return bearing; for bearings less than 180, add 180 degrees to arrive at the correct return bearing. For example, an original bearing of 30 degrees from point A to point B would mean a return bearing of 210 degrees from point B to point A. An original bear-

Figure 3-15

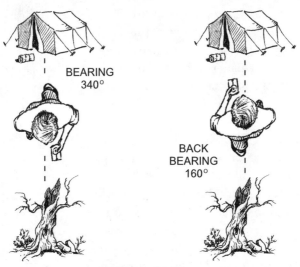

Figure 3-16

ing of 220 degrees from point A to point B would give you a return bearing of 40 degrees. Make sense? Kinda makes you wish you'd paid more attention to Mr. Frumplemeyer when he was outlining those math formulas in ninth grade, now, doesn't it?

Navigating When There Aren't Landmarks

There will come a time when landmarks disappear beneath a shroud of fog, or are masked by a dense forest, or disappear altogether as you make your way across a featureless plain, snowfield, or desert. Working your way along a course under these conditions is challenging but not impossible. It does require a tremendous amount of patience, however. If you have a partner, all the better. Assuming you have established your bearing as described above, use your partner as the intermediate landmark. Point your direction-of-travel arrow ahead and have your hiking partner head off in that direction. Stay in visual contact at all times. Before your partner disappears from sight, have her stop and turn around to face you. It's essential that you line her up *exactly* with the imaginary beam the arrow is sending toward the invisible landmark. Move her to the right or left with hand signals until she's exactly in place. Now hike toward her.

What happens if you're alone? Things get more difficult, though

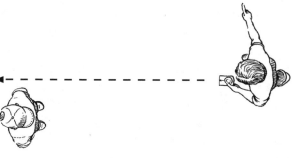

Figure 3-17

not impossible. Get ready to back-sight like mad. Before you head off along the bearing indicated by your direction-of-travel arrow, erect a visible monument at the point you're now standing. It can be a large branch propped up so it's visible from a distance, or sev-eral rocks stacked one on top of the other—it doesn't matter so long as it's visible and natural. Don't needlessly mar the landscape. Hike off from your landmark, stopping just before you lose sight of it. Take a back-bearing and place yourself on course by mov-ing right or left until your magnetic needle is boxed by the orienting arrow and the direction-of-travel arrow is pointing exactly at your monument. Turn around, set up another monu-ment to your travels, and head off again. It will take you a while, but you'll eventually get where you want to go.

Using the Night Sky

Celestial Navigation Using the North Star

Yes, navigating by Polaris (also known as the North Star) does require a clear view of the sky and an ability to iden-

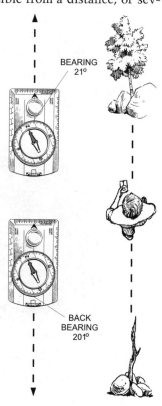

Figure 3-18

tify at least one star formation—the Big Dipper—but assuming you can pick out that constellation, you can determine which way is north. The beauty of the North Star is that it stays in one place in the sky, and always to the north of you. To pick it out of the mass of other twinkling stars, find the Big Dipper, then look to the two stars that make up the side of the dipper's ladle. The North Star lies above these two stars, known as pointer stars, in a relatively straight line, approximately four to six times the distance between the pointer stars.

How does this help you? Well, if you consider that a compass is nothing more than a circle with north at the top, south at the bottom, east to the right, and west to the left, you can draw a crude circle in the soil and mark off the cardinal reference points (N, S, E, W) based on the north end of the circle pointing directly at the North Star. If you have a map, you can now orient it fairly accurately and get a good read of the land. Don't have a map? Whoops! Don't panic, though. You can still navigate by using the North Star to maintain your sense of direction and prevent yourself from hiking in circles, wasting valuable time and energy.

Figure 3-19

What about Celestial Navigation in the Southern Hemisphere?

Unfortunately, it isn't as easy as in the Northern Hemisphere, chiefly because there's no clearly visible star whose position remains firmly fixed in the sky, like the North Star. Still, it is possible—using a little careful estimation and visualization—to navigate by the stars. First of all, you must locate the Southern Cross. The upright, or longest section, of the cross is made up of four clearly visible stars, with a fifth, much fainter star resting just off center. If your eyes can follow a line through this longer section of the cross to a point approximately four and a half times its length, you will arrive at a point where a "South Star" would be if it existed. Find a landmark directly below this point. That will become your south reference point.

Create a roughly drawn compass in the soil, as noted above, so that when the sun rises you'll still be able to determine which way is south—and then, hopefully, which way you should be heading.

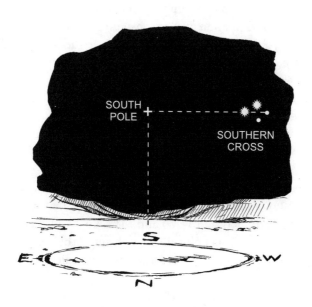

Figure 3-20

Using a Watch to Tell Direction

Northern Hemisphere

Even if you don't have a watch, you can establish a good sense of
direction as long as you can see the sun. I've determined the sun's
position, even on a hazy day, by being able to locate the glowing
orb hidden behind a veil of clouds. If you're wearing
a watch with an hour hand and are sure it's set
to the correct local time, then the going is
simple. By holding the watch level, turn
yourself until the hour hand points in
the direction of the sun. Establish a
point on your watch that's one half
the distance between the hour hand
and 12:00. The north-south line runs
from this point—halfway between the
hour hand and 12:00—and the center
of the watch. North is the point on the
line farthest from the sun.

SOUTH

NORTH

Figure 3-21

Not wearing a watch, or your watch is
digital? No worries, mate, as long as you have a
relatively good imagination and are absolutely sure of the time.
Imagine that you're wearing a watch and place the hour hand in
the correct position for the time of day. Now follow the directions
in the paragraph above and you'll find yourself facing the same
direction. Keep in mind that neither method is 100 percent accurate; still, either offers a good-enough fix to help you navigate.

Southern Hemisphere

If you're south of the equator and your watch is again set to the
correct local time, vary the above-described technique somewhat
by aiming 12:00 directly at the sun. Establish a point on the watch
face that's halfway between 12:00 and the hour hand. The north-
south line runs from this point directly through the center of the
watch. The point on the line closest to the sun indicates north.

Let the Shadows Point the Way

Did you ever attempt to make a sundial when you were a child?

Telling the time was possible only if a bright sun created a good shadow. Well, determining east and west from shadows cast by the sun is no different, really—you just need a bright sun and a large-enough stick to create a good shadow.

Push a straight stick into the ground as vertically as possible. Place a pebble or scratch a mark at the end-point where the shadow is cast. Now, if you have a watch, time about thirty minutes; without a watch, spend your minutes counting out half an hour— "one one-thousand, two one-thousand," and so on. After approximately thirty minutes have passed, place another pebble or scratch another mark at the second endpoint of the shadow. Now draw a straight line connecting the two points. This line is pointing approximately east-west, with west being to the left and east to the right as you face the stick.

Figure 3-22

Working Your Way Around Obstacles

What happens if you come to a natural obstacle you hadn't counted on, an obstacle that stands directly in your path and established compass bearing? No problem! The easiest solution is to select a landmark on the other side of the obstacle—assuming that your obstacle is something flat, such as a lake or a wide swamp. Work your way around the lake to the landmark, take a back-sighting to be sure you're actually back on course, and then proceed. However, if the obstacle is a massive cliff and there's no way to establish a visible landmark on the other side in line with your established route of travel, you must opt for option two—just hike around it, using measured steps and maintaining a calculated bear-

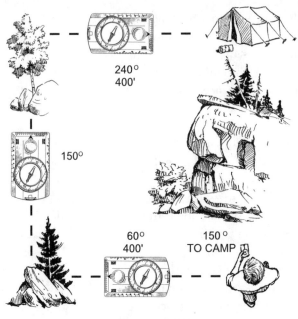

240°
400'

150°

60°
400'

150°
TO CAMP

Figure 3-23

ing and keeping your changes in course as close to absolute right-angled (90-degree) turns as possible.

Once you arrive at the obstacle, keep the compass direction-of-travel arrow pointing at your intended direction, but turn and face to the right or left. You should now be holding the compass so that you're able to sight along its back edge, with the arrow pointing directly off toward your right or left. Walk as straight a line as possible toward a distant landmark established by sighting off the back edge of the baseplate. Walk carefully and count your steps exactly. Once you're around the obstacle and can resume heading in the correct direction, turn and resume walking in line with the direction-of-travel arrow. Keep in mind, however, that you're now off course, although heading in the correct direction. To get back on course, you need to head back in the opposite direction once you're around the obstacle. To do this, again turn your body so that you're able to sight along the back edge of the compass base-plate and establish a landmark to hike toward. Now hike in a straight line, counting steps again. Stop hiking when you've walked exactly the number of steps you counted before. At this point turn back into line with the direction-of-travel arrow and resume hiking. Now you're not only heading in the correct direction but back on course as well.

Caring for Your Compass

Although your compass is built to take a licking and keep on pointing, a little TLC for your navigational friend is well advised. For starters, try not to drop it or let it bang against hard surfaces—if you let a compass hang loosely around your neck from a lanyard, it's liable to whack against hard objects that do it no good. I tuck my compass inside my shirt to protect it when it's hanging around my neck and not in use. If you have a sighting compass with a cover, keep it closed when not in use. I also recommend that you purchase a nylon or leather sheath for your compass for additional protection when you're carrying it in a pack or pocket.

Never leave your compass sitting in an extremely hot environment, such as on a rock under intense desert sun or on the dashboard or in the glove compartment of your car. Extreme temperatures can cause the damping fluid in your compass to rupture the housing and leak out, rendering the instrument useless.

Keep your compass away from high-intensity magnetic fields, such as electromagnets (electric motors, for example); they can temporarily disorient or even permanently demagnetize the compass needle. Your compass won't be much good to you if the formerly magnetized needle wanders aimlessly just when you're counting on it to point you in the right direction.

While insect repellents are often essential to thwart the attacks of mosquitoes, blackflies, midges, and ticks, the chemicals in repellents (typically deet) can, and most often will, eat the ink right off your compass housing. Worse, deet has been known to affect the plastic housing of a compass, causing it to cloud up and even crack—major bummer. Be sure to clean your hands thoroughly before touching your compass.

Over time the needle on your compass may begin to act sluggishly, or even seem to stick to the bottom of the liquid-filled housing. This is usually due to a buildup of static electricity within the housing. Correct it by simply rubbing a small amount of water directly over the housing to disperse the static charge.

It's not uncommon for a small bubble to appear in the liquid-filled housing when you're using your compass at high elevations or in below-freezing temperatures. The bubble forms because the fluid within the housing contracts or expands at a faster rate than the housing, resulting in a "vacuum" bubble. This bubble will not affect the performance of your compass, because the liquid's sole purpose is to dampen or slow down the movement of the magnetic needle. Typically, any bubble will disappear when the compass is returned to room temperature or lower elevation. If the bubble remains, you can correct the situation by placing the compass in a warm (not hot) spot, such as a sunny windowsill. Do keep an eye on the bubble if it refuses to depart. Should the bubble grow in size, you might have a small, almost imperceptible leak in the liquid-filled compass housing. That means you need a new compass.

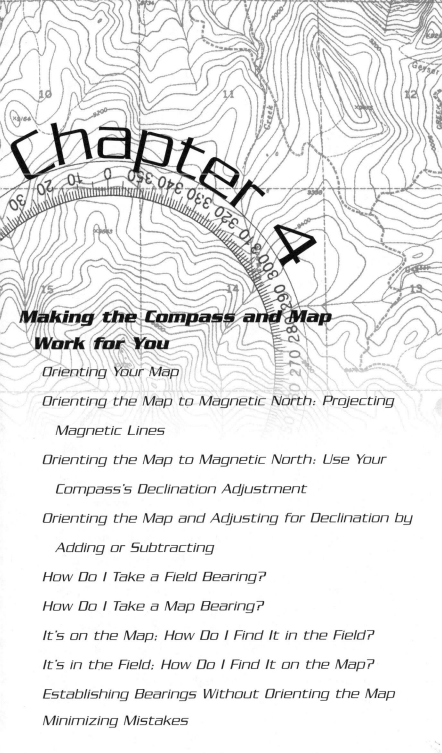

Chapter 4

Making the Compass and Map Work for You

Making the Compass and Map Work for You

Orienting Your Map

A map represents the lay of the land, so if you with to match the geographic picture with the map image, you must accurately orient your map to the lay of the land. You can do this by picking out landmarks and then spinning your map to match those land-marks—assuming your map-reading skills and your geographic-interpretation skills are good enough. Still, geographic orientation is only roughly accurate, even with the best observation. For absolute accuracy you must turn to your compass. It will help you orient the map so it becomes an exact mirror image of the terrain around you.

Since the map is printed with the edge lined up with true north and your compass needle always points toward magnetic north, you'll have to account for declination to correctly align your map. As I discussed in the previous chapters, the difference between the north shown on a topographic map and the north indicated by the magnetic needle on your compass is known as declination. Declination is either west or east, depending on which side of the geographic north your compass needle points. On USGS topographic maps declination is indicated by arrows printed on the bottom margin. The arrow with a star above it indicates true or geographic north. The shorter arrow with an MN above it indicates magnetic north. The number with the degree sign printed between the two arrows is the exact degree of declination (Figure 4-1; see also appendix Figure A-6).

There are several ways to ensure accuracy. First, you can orient the map simply by drawing magnetic lines across it that parallel the declination angle (in essence, you're adjusting the map to magnetic compass speak). This is my favorite method: Once the magnetic lines are drawn, the magnetic needle, its orienting arrow, and the map are all speaking the same language, minimizing the possibility for field errors. The disadvantage of this method is that you

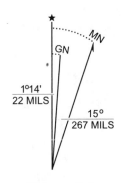

Figure 4-1

have to draw magnetic lines across all the maps you plan to use in the field, and you must draw them very accurately using a protractor, a perfectly straight yardstick, and a relatively flat surface.

In my opinion the next best method—and a very close second to the first—is adjusting your compass to the declination indicated on the map (this time adjusting the compass to true-north map speak). The advantage of this method is that once your compass is adjusted—assuming you have a built-in declination adjustment feature, which is worth the few extra dollars you'll spend to get it—you can forget about having to compensate for declination as long as you remain on that map. All you have to do is turn a screw, spin a dial, or adjust a scale—no drawing of lines whatsoever. The disadvantage is that you'll have to remember to adjust your setting when moving to adjacent maps with possibly different declinations—a very minor disadvantage, to be sure.

The third method involves the magic of numbers and mathematical calculation of the declination—not just when you're orienting the map, but also when you're taking bearings from the map or the field. If you are to be a well-rounded and skilled navigator, it's essential that you understand this method, although I personally hate it and rarely rely on it. Why? Because when you're fatigued, stressed, anxious, or hurried, numbers add a distraction that can become quite confusing, dramatically increasing the possibility of error.

Orienting the Map to True North: Projecting Magnetic Lines

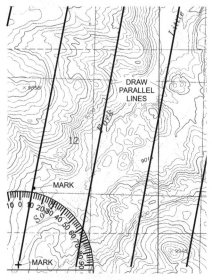

Figure 4-2

A common way to make the process of adjusting for declination easy is to use a protractor, a yardstick with a very straight edge, and a pencil to project the declination line across the entire topo. Your first step is to mark a point along the bottom border of the map and then place the center point of the protractor directly on your mark. Make another mark at the degree bearing indicated by the declination angle, being sure that your angle is facing the same way as the declination dia-

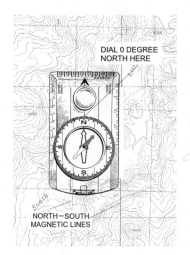

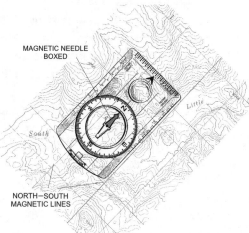

Figure 4-3 Orienting Map with Magnetic Lines. Dial 0 degree north into direction-of-travel arrow (index line). Place edge of compass on drawn magnetic lines. Without moving compass, rotate map until magnetic needle is boxed with orienting arrow.

gram. For example, a 10-degree declination to the east (the MN arrow is to the right of the arrow with the star above it) means you count 10 degrees to the right of the 0-degree marking on the protractor, placing a mark at 10 degrees. Now connect the two points and project the line all the way across the map using the yardstick. Finally, using this line as a guide, you can draw parallel magnetic-north lines 1 to 2 inches apart (Figure 4-2). Take the compass with the orienting arrow pointing due north, place the edge of the baseplate along one of the magnetic lines, and spin the map until the magnetic arrow is centered (boxed) within the orienting arrow (Figure 4-3).

Orienting the Map to True North: Using Your Compass's Declination Adjustment

No magnetic lines on your map? Then the next easiest method is to adjust your compass to the declination, which is simple if your compass features a built-in declination adjustment. Each manufacturer has a different way to accomplish this, so refer to the instructions that came with your compass. All methods accomplish the same thing, however. By moving the orienting arrow to the right of north (for east declination) or to the left of north (for west declination), the compass will read true or geographic north (Figure 4-4). To orient the map, place the edge of the compass baseplate along the printed edge of the map, then spin the map until the red end of the magnetic needle is centered (boxed) in the orienting arrow. Your map is now oriented to magnetic north. You will note that the north–south line of your compass and the direction-of-travel arrow parallel the edge of your map to indicate true north, while the magnetic needle continues to point

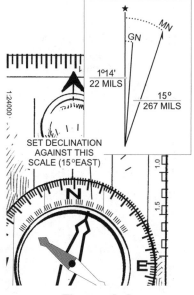

Figure 4-4

to indicate true north, while the magnetic needle continues to point east or west, matching the angle of declination indicated by the map's declination diagram—nifty, isn't it? Once your compass is set, you won't have to readjust the declination as long as you're navigating within the boundaries of that map. Don't forget, however, that as you move from map to map and region to region, the declination will change; you'll have to adjust the compass accordingly each time (Figure 4-5).

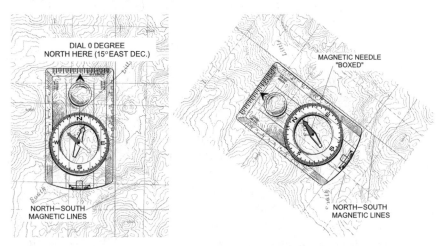

Figure 4-5 Orienting Map with Adjustable Declination Compass. Adjust compass for declination, dialing 0 degree north with direction-of-travel arrow (index line). Place compass along north–south line on map. Without moving compass, rotate map until magnetic needle is boxed with orienting arrow.

Orienting the Map and Adjusting for Declination by Adding or Subtracting

If you don't have a compass that features a built-in declination adjustment, you'll have to resort to turning the compass housing to compensate for the declination before each attempt to orient your map. If the MN arrow is on the left side of the true-north arrow, the declination is west and you turn the housing to the left (counterclockwise), counting each degree until north sits the designated number of degrees of declination to the right of the index point (10 degrees of west declination means you turn the housing until 10 degrees is indicated opposite the compass's index point: 360 degrees (north) + 10 degrees = 10 degrees. How did I get 10 degrees by adding 10 to 360? Remember that a compass is a 360-degree circle. You can't go higher than 360 degrees no matter how hard you try. So when you're adding to 360 degrees, you are, in actual fact, adding to 0 degrees and continuing around the circle to the right. If the MN arrow is on the right side of the true-north arrow, the declination is east and you turn the housing to the right (clockwise), counting each degree until north sits the designated number of degrees of declination to the left of the index point (10 degrees of east declination means you turn the housing until 350 degrees is indicated opposite the compass's index point: 360 degrees (north) - 10 degrees = 350 degrees (Figure 4-6).

Should you opt for this method, realize that you aren't done with Math 101 just because your map is successfully oriented. Anytime you take a bearing from the map to the compass or field or from the compass or field to the map, you'll have to convert the reading so that it compensates for declination. How?

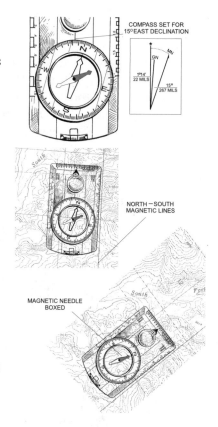

Figure 4-6 Determine declination and add or subtract from north on azimuth. This figure demonstrates a 15-degree east declination. Fifteen degrees less 360 degrees, equals 345 degrees. Rotate azimuth ring until degree declination difference north on azimuth is aligned with the direction-of-travel arrow. Place edge of compass along north–south line on map. Make sure direction-of-travel arrow is pointing toward the north end of map. Without moving the compass, rotate map until needle is "boxed" with orienting arrow.

To compensate for declination when you're taking a reading from the map that you want to use in the field, you must do the following: If the MN arrow is on the left side of the true-north arrow, the declination is west and you add the indicated degree amount to correct your bearing. If the MN arrow is on the right side of the true-north arrow, the declination is east and you subtract the indicated degree amount to correct your bearing.

To compensate for declination when taking a reading from the field that you want to use on the map, do the following; If the MN arrow is on the left side of the true-north arrow, the declination is west; subtract the indicated degree amount to correct your bearing. If the MN arrow is on the right side of the true-north arrow, the declination is east; add the indicated degree amount to correct your bearing (Figure 4-7).

Say what? It's really not as hard as it sounds. If your indicated heading is 80 degrees after taking a map bearing, and the map declination is 10 degrees east, turn your bezel 10 degrees east, subtracting the degrees, to leave you with a corrected bearing of 70 degrees.

Why is this important? In this example, if you didn't correct for declination and set off hiking on an 80-degree bearing, you would be off course by approximately 0.2 mile (920 feet) for each mile traveled (for each degree of error, you'll be approximately 18.4 feet off course for every 1,056 feet traveled)—no wonder you can't find that freshwater spring!

20°WEST DECLINATION

20°EAST DECLINATION

Figure 4-7 Rotate azimuth ring 15 degrees east of 0 degree north to adjust for declination. Place compass along north–south line on map. Without moving compass, rotate map until magnetic needle is boxed with orienting arrow.

Declination Error Example Chart

Declination Error	Distance Traveled	Distance Off Course
1 degree	1 mile	92 feet
1 degree	5 miles	460 feet
1 degree	10 miles	921 feet (approx. 0.2 mile)
2 degrees	1 mile	184 feet
2 degrees	5 miles	921 feet (approx 0.2 mile)
2 degrees	10 miles	1,844 feet (approx. 0.3 mile)
5 degrees	1 mile	461 feet
5 degrees	5 miles	2,309 feet (approx. 0.5 mile)
5 degrees	10 miles	4,619 feet (approx. 0.8 mile)
10 degrees	1 mile	931 feet (approx. 0.2 mile)
10 degrees	5 miles	4,655 feet (approx. 0.8 mile)
10 degrees	10 miles	9,310 feet (approx. 1.75 miles)
20 degrees	1 mile	1,921 feet (approx. 0.3 mile)
20 degrees	5 miles	9,608 feet (approx. 1.8 miles)
20 degrees	10 miles	19,219 feet (approx. 3.7 miles)

How Do I Take a Field Bearing?

Imagine that you're hiking toward a distant mountain peak that's presently visible from the ridge you're on, but you know that you'll soon lose sight of it in the woods. How can you be sure you'll stay on course? Hold your compass level at waist height and point the direction-of-travel arrow at the mountain peak. Rotate the compass housing until the red end of the magnetic compass needle is centered (boxed) within the orienting arrow. Your bearing may be read in degrees at the center index point—where the compass housing meets the direction-of-travel arrow on the compass baseplate.

To follow that bearing, pick the first major landmark in line with the direction-of-travel arrow (say a large evergreen)—one that you

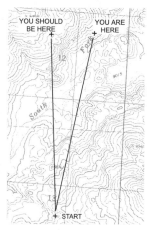

Figure 4-8

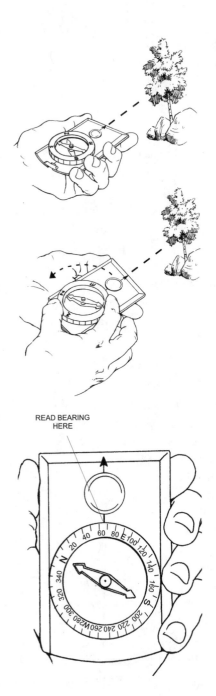

READ BEARING
HERE

won't lose sight of once you're into the woods. Also, look over your shoulder and select a major landmark (say a rocky outcrop) directly behind you—again, one you won't lose sight of. Do not touch that compass dial! Walk directly toward the evergreen and don't worry that you can no longer see the mountain peak, because your compass reading has already been set at the index. Once you're at the tree, hold the compass level once again, turn your body until the north end of the compass needle centers itself exactly inside the orienting arrow, and then find another landmark in line with the direction-of-travel arrow. Before you head out, take a back bearing by turning around with the compass still held level until the white end of the compass needle is centered inside the orienting arrow. Do you see the rocky outcrop in line with the direction-of-travel arrow? If so, you're on course for the mountain peak as planned. Turn around and head directly to your next selected landmark. Repeat the process until you arrive at your selected destination, the mountain peak (Figure 4-9).

Figure 4-9 Field Bearing. Hold compass level with travel arrow pointing toward landmark. Rotate housing and box magnetic needle with orienting arrow. Read bearing at index line.

How Do I Take a Map Bearing?

Oh, oh. You still want to head to that mountain peak, but this time you're enshrouded in dense fog. How are you going to get there? First, orient your map. Now, place the edge of the baseplate like a ruler with the direction-of-travel arrow pointing from your current location on the map toward your intended destination. The edge of the baseplate should exactly connect your current location and your intended destination. Being careful not to move either the map or the compass, rotate the compass housing until the north end of the compass needle centers itself exactly inside the orienting arrow. Your degree bearing is indicated at the index point. Now, without moving the compass housing, stand up—holding the compass level at your waist—and rotate your body until the north end of the compass needle centers itself exactly inside the orienting arrow. Your course is indicated by the direction-of-travel arrow (Figure 4-10). Follow the navigation directions above for taking a field bearing.

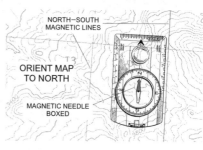

NORTH–SOUTH MAGNETIC LINES

ORIENT MAP TO NORTH

MAGNETIC NEEDLE BOXED

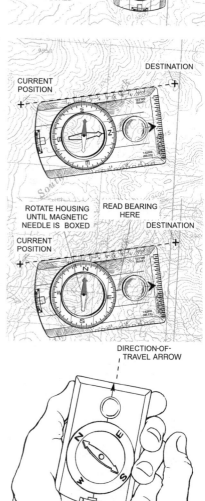

DESTINATION

CURRENT POSITION

ROTATE HOUSING UNTIL MAGNETIC NEEDLE IS BOXED

READ BEARING HERE

DESTINATION

CURRENT POSITION

DIRECTION-OF-TRAVEL ARROW

Figure 4-10 Map Bearing. Orient map. Place edge of compass connecting current location with destination. Make sure direction-of-travel arrow is pointing toward destination. Rotate housing to box magnetic needle with orienting arrow. Read bearing at index line. Hold compass level and rotate body until needle is boxed with orienting arrow.

It's on the Map; How Do I Find It in the Field?

You can see where you are on the map, that much is certain. You've even picked out an interesting summit on the map, not too far from where you are now, and you want to explore it. But in scanning the terrain, you're having a hard time picking the summit out of the several others clustered nearby. What do you do? Follow the directions for taking a map bearing. Once you have the established bearing and have rotated your body, holding the compass at waist level until the magnetic needle is boxed or centered within the orienting arrow, you should be able to determine which summit you want—it's the one the direction-if-travel arrow is pointing toward (Figure 4-11).

Figure 4-11 Find in Field. Orient map. Place edge of compass connecting current location with destination. Make sure direction-of-travel arrow is pointing toward destination. Rotate housing to box magnetic needle with orienting arrow. Read bearing at index line. Hold compass level and rotate body until needle is boxed with orienting arrow. Direction-of-travel arrow is pointing at landmark.

It's in the Field; How Do I Find It on the Map?

You can see that distant summit, and you know where you are on the map, but you have no idea which summit on the map is the one you're looking at in the field. What's a navigator to do? First, orient your map. Then hold your compass level at waist height and point the direction-of-travel arrow at the mountain's summit. Rotate the compass housing until the red end of the magnetic compass needle is centered (boxed) within the orienting arrow. Your bearing can be read in degrees at the center index point—where the compass housing meets the direction-of-travel arrow on the compass baseplate. Taking care not to move the map, place one edge of the compass's baseplate directly on your current location on the map. Now,

NORTH–SOUTH
MAGNETIC LINES

ORIENT MAP
TO NORTH

MAGNETIC NEEDLE
BOXED

CURRENT
POSITION

Figure 4-12 Find on Map. Orient map. Hold compass level and sight to landmark. Rotate compass housing and box magnetic needle with orienting arrow. Place compass edge on present location. Rotate compass while leaving edge on present location until needle is boxed with orienting arrow. Draw line from landmark.

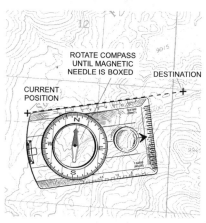

ROTATE COMPASS
UNTIL MAGNETIC
NEEDLE IS BOXED

DESTINATION

CURRENT
POSITION

without moving the compass housing or moving the map in any way, pivot the compass around your known location point until the red end of the magnetic compass needle is centered (boxed) within the orienting arrow. Draw a line, either in pencil or in your imagination, along the edge of the baseplate toward the summits indicated on the map. The summit you're looking at in the field will be the one intersected by the line drawn from your location (Figure 4-12).

Establishing Bearings without Orienting the Map

Do you always have to orient a map to establish a bearing? No, although keep in mind that anytime you don't orient the map, you're increasing the opportunity for error. Still, these techniques are especially useful when you're trying to establish a bearing on the fly and you don't want to take the time to orient the map. What I most like about this technique is that you can accurately plan your entire trip at home, establishing correct bearings and then writing those bearings down to use when you actually head out into the field. Here's how to follow these "no-map-orientation-needed" procedures (Figure 4-13).

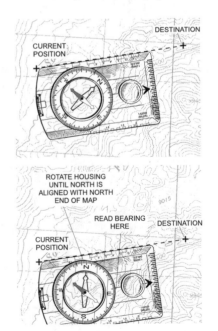

Figure 4-13 Map Bearing without Orienting Map. Place edge of compass connecting current location with destination. Make sure direction-of-travel arrow is pointing toward destination. Rotate housing until north end of azimuth ring is pointing toward north end of map. Read bearing at index line.

For a Map with Magnetic Lines Projected Across It

If you have magnetic lines drawn on your map, do not use your compass's built-in declination adjustment.

To Establish a Bearing from the Map (Map to Field): Connect your location with your destination, using the edge of your compass baseplate with the direction-of-travel arrow pointing toward your destination. Being careful not to move the compass, rotate its housing until the orienting arrow points to magnetic north (if you don't do this correctly and end up pointing the orienting arrow south, your bearing will be 180 degrees off) and the compass housing's orienting lines parallel the map's magnetic-northlines. Ignore the magnetic needle entirely. Your bearing can be read at the index point (Figure 4-14).

To Plot a Bearing on the Map (Field to Map): After establishing your field bearing, do not move the dial. Place one edge of the compass on your known point on the map (if you know your location, place the bottom corner of the baseplate on your location with the direction-of-travel arrow pointing away; if you know a landmark but your location is unverified, place the top corner of

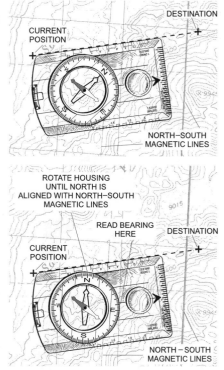

Figure 4-14 Map Bearing with Magnetic Lines. Place edge of compass connecting current location with destination. Make sure direction-of-travel arrow is pointing toward destination. Rotate housing until orienting arrow aligns with magnetic lines. Read bearing at index line.

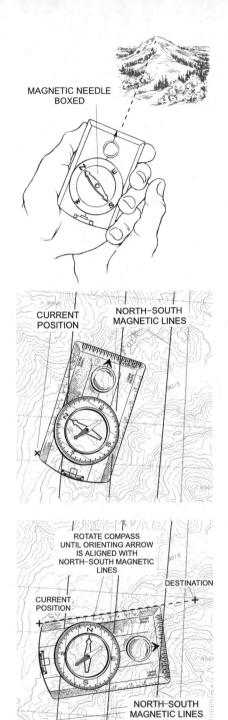

MAGNETIC NEEDLE
BOXED

CURRENT
POSITION

NORTH–SOUTH
MAGNETIC LINES

ROTATE COMPASS
UNTIL ORIENTING ARROW
IS ALIGNED WITH
NORTH–SOUTH MAGNETIC
LINES

DESTINATION

CURRENT
POSITION

NORTH–SOUTH
MAGNETIC LINES

the baseplate on the landmark, direction-of-travel
arrow pointing at the landmark). Rotate the entire compass around the point until
you align the orienting lines
with the magnetic lines projected on your map. Draw a
line on the map along the
edge of the baseplate from
your known point out; that's
your bearing, plotted on the
map (Figure 4-15).

For a Map with No Magnetic Lines, Relying on the Border

If you don't have magnetic
lines drawn on your map, use
the printed edge of the map
or the grid lines projected
across it. If your map doesn't
have grid lines, you need to
either extend a straight line
from your location, through
your destination, and to
either the right or left printed
edge of the map; or draw

Figure 4-15 Field to Map
with Magnetic Lines. Hold compass level and sight to landmark.
Rotate compass housing and box
magnetic needle with orienting
arrow. Place compass edge on
present location. Rotate compass
while leaving edge on present
location until orienting arrow
aligns with magnetic line. Draw
line from landmark.

lines on the map that parallel its printed edge. You also need to compensate for declination, which is most easily accomplished by using a compass with a built-in declination adjustment.

To Establish a Bearing from the Map (Map to Field): Draw a straight line on the map that connects your location with your destination and extends through either the right (east) or left (west) edge of the map. Place the edge of your compass's baseplate with the direction-of-travel arrow positioned so that it's pointing in the same direction as your direction of travel would be on the map, from location to destination. Being careful not to move the compass, rotate the compass housing until the orienting lines are aligned with map's printed border or grid lines. Ignore the magnetic needle entirely. Your bearing can be read at the index point (Figure 4-16).

To Plot a Bearing on the Map (Field to Map): After establishing your field bearing, do not move the dial. Place one edge of the compass on your known point on the map (if you know your location, place the bottom corner of the baseplate on your location with the direction-of-travel arrow pointing away; if you know a landmark but your location is unverified, place the

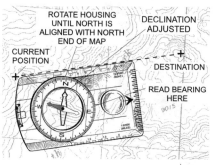

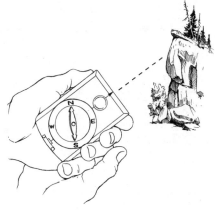

Figure 4-16 Map to Field without Magnetic Lines. Adjust compass for declination. Place edge of compass connecting current location with destination. Make sure direction-of-travel arrow is pointing toward destination. Rotate housing until orienting arrow aligns with north end of map. Read bearing at index line. Adjust declination before sighting bearing.

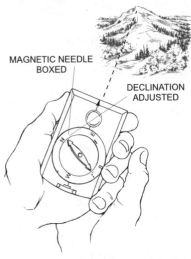

MAGNETIC NEEDLE
BOXED

DECLINATION
ADJUSTED

CURRENT
POSITION

×

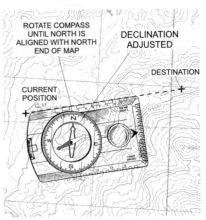

ROTATE COMPASS
UNTIL NORTH IS
ALIGNED WITH NORTH
END OF MAP

DECLINATION
ADJUSTED

DESTINATION

CURRENT
POSITION

top corner of the baseplate on the landmark, direction-of-travel arrow pointing at the landmark). Rotate the entire compass around the point until you align the orienting lines with the printed border of the map or the grid lines on your map. Draw a line on the map along the edge of the baseplate; and that's your bearing on the map (Figure 4-17).

Minimizing Mistakes

I have learned over the years, and the lesson was reinforced not long ago during the Eco-Challenge, that even the most experienced navigator can make a mistake if he is not careful. Military cadets have been known to call in air strikes on their own platoon because of navigational errors— fortunately, this has occurred in practice sessions when personnel are afforded eternal life. Adventure racers head off in the wrong direction because fatigue inspired them to miss a critical step or mis-

Figure 4-17 Field to Map without Magnetic Lines. Adjust compass for declination. Hold compass level and sight to landmark. Rotate compass housing and box magnetic needle with orienting arrow. Place compass edge on present location. Rotate compass while leaving edge on present location until orienting arrow aligns with north end of map.

read a compass. One sleep-deprived navigator in a recent Eco-Challenge was discovered holding his compass the wrong way, with the direction-of-travel arrow pointing directly at himself.

Always double-check yourself and stay ever vigilant so that you do not do the following:

- Adjust for declination in the wrong direction.
- Miscalculate the declination correction.
- Try to follow a long leg on a bearing without accounting for drift—always hike from visible point to visible point to stay on course.
- Travel with the map and compass put away because "you know where you are." Always check your position with regularity.
- Hold a compass next to a metal object, such as a belt buckle, when trying to take a bearing.
- Take sloppy bearings. Always use the same eye and check your sighting two or three times.
- Incorrectly draw the magnetic lines on a map.
- Get confused and use the wrong end of the magnetic needle.
- Get confused and read the bearing from the opposite side of the index point.
- Point the direction-of-travel arrow in the wrong direction when you're establishing a bearing.

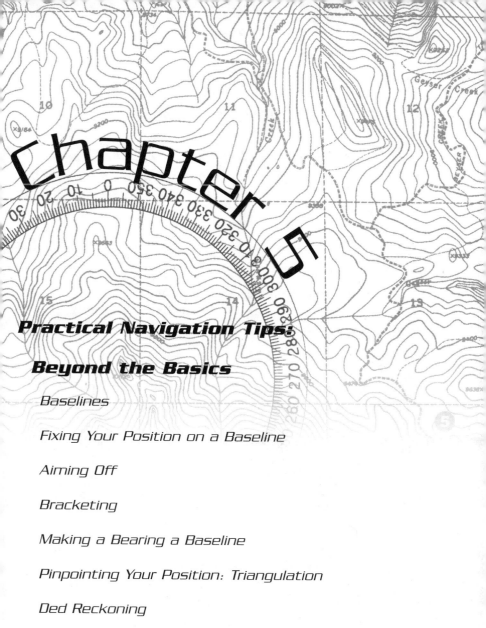

Chapter 5

Practical Navigation Tips:

Beyond the Basics

Practical Navigation
Tips: Beyond the Basics

Now that you've learned the meat-and-potatoes techniques that every navigator uses regularly to be successful in finding her way, it's time to move on to the more advanced skills.

Baselines

In the field baselines come into play on a regular basis as you seek to find your way. A baseline is a long line that can easily be identified and used as a point of reference on a map. A river, trail, fence line, power line, railway, road, river, or even a long and easily identifiable ridge can serve as a baseline (Figure 5-1). When two identifiable baselines intersect, that provides an indisputable reference point on the map. Even if you've never stepped onto a trail, I'll bet you've used baselines in giving directions to your home or a meeting place in the city. "Stay on First Street [one baseline] until you hit Meridian [another baseline] and turn left. Follow Meridian to Broadway [yet another baseline] and turn right. Drive 1 mile and my house is on the right." The practice remains the same in the field. "Hike 2 miles on the Tuolomne Trail from Bear Lake Campground until you arrive at the Twin Summits Trail. Turn right and hike until Twin Summits crosses Sparkling Creek. Our campground will be in the meadow just north of the crossing on the left side of the trail."

Skiers, hikers, and hunters frequently use baselines when heading out into the woods to explore, especially when leaving a camp or a vehicle next to a road or trail. The beauty of a good baseline is that you don't really have to keep detailed tabs on your particular course. If your camp is sitting next to a river that runs generally east–west, you could head off to the south or north, explore for a while, reverse your direction, and be assured that you'll once again arrive at the baseline—in this case, the river. No real navigational headaches here. There is, however, one minor question: Once you get to the baseline (the river), should you head north or south to get back to camp: This may seem like a tough question to answer if you haven't been paying close attention to your wanderings. But fortunately, there are several easy ways to solve this dilemma without having to resort to the time- and energy-sapping method of trial and error.

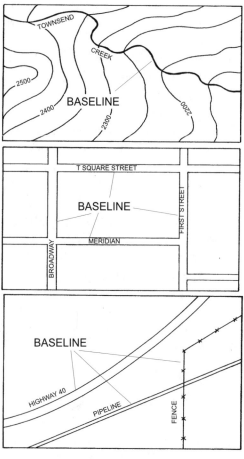

Figure 5-1

Fixing Your Position on a Baseline

So you've arrived back at the river and have no idea which way to turn? No problem. First, orient your map. Then, standing next to the baseline (the river), take a bearing on a distant and recognizable landmark. To do this, hold your compass level at waist height and point the direction-of-travel arrow at the landmark. Rotate the compass housing until the red end of the magnetic compass needle is centered (boxed) within the orienting arrow. Your bearing can be read in degrees at the center index point—where the compass housing meets the direction-of-travel arrow on the compass baseplate. Taking care not to move the map, place one edge of the compass baseplate directly on the landmark, with the direction-of-travel arrow pointing from the baseline (river) toward the landmark. Now, without moving the compass housing or moving the map in any way, pivot the compass around the landmark point until the red end of the magnetic compass needle is centered (boxed) within the orienting arrow. Draw a line, either in pencil or in your imagination, along the edge of the baseplate until it intersects with the baseline (river) you're standing beside. Your location on the river is where the two lines intersect. Assuming you know where your camp is on the river, you should know whether to head east or west to return to your shelter (Figure 5-2).

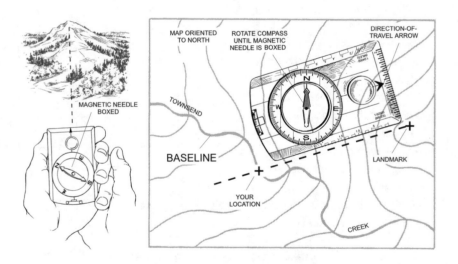

Figure 5-2 **Finding Yourself with Baseline.** Orient map. Hold compass level and sight to landmark. Rotate compass housing and box magnetic needle with orienting arrow. Place compass edge on landmark sighted. Rotate compass while leaving edge on landmark until needle is boxed with orienting arrow. Draw line from landmark. Location is where baseline and bearing intersect.

Aiming Off

Another way to find your camp along the river is to intentionally miss the camp so far to the north or south that you'll know which way to head. In other words, make your mistake so bad that it becomes an intentional error you can correct once you arrive at the river. For instance, you wandered well away from camp in a generally northerly direction and want to head back. You're somewhat sure where the

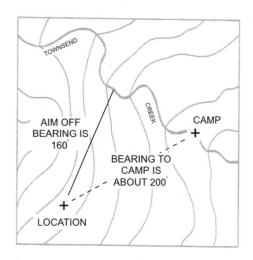

Figure 5-3

camp lies—you can see a saddle in a distant ridge behind you and know your camp is somewhere below that. The problem is, if you head toward the saddle and arrive at the river, will you arrive just east or just west of the camp? You have no way of knowing. The solution: Pick a route that will position you well east of the saddle. That way, once you arrive at the baseline (river), you'll know for certain that camp lies to the west. Now all you do is hike along the river until you reach camp. Simple!

Bracketing

This technique, frequently used by hunters, wildlife watchers, and fishers, involves a little more detailed analysis of your location along a baseline. Called bracketing, it's especially useful when you leave a vehicle parked alongside a remote forest service road. A bracket is nothing more than an identifiable boundary that lets you know you should turn around and head the other way on a baseline to get to your destination. A bracket is also useful in helping you determine if the baseline you're on is actually the baseline you want; this is extremely valuable when wandering the mountains of the West, where the forests are crisscrossed with forest service roads that look decidedly similar.

I frequently use brackets when I leave my vehicle beside a remote road to go backcountry skiing. On the drive in I'll identify one landmark that I know is about 0.5 mile from where I want to park, and then another one within 0.25 mile, and one more within a few hundred yards. Most often I drive past my parking area to establish similar brackets in the other direction. If the road is blocked to vehicles but continues on, I'll head off on my skis to establish the brackets before I dare head away from the road. Brackets can be bridges, road signs, rockfalls, large boulders, deadfalls, a large and recognizable tree, and the like. Forget trying to remember the brackets. Instead, record them meticulously on a sheet of paper. Once I return from my skiing to the road, I use the brackets to tell me which way to turn to get back to my vehicle.

Making a Bearing a Baseline

You're camping in the desert and there are no rivers, fence lines, roads, trails, or anything else that you can see fit to use as a physical baseline. Nev-ertheless, you want to go off exploring, and you'd like to be reasonably sure you can return to camp without difficulty. What do you do? When there isn't a baseline to be had, make your own. No, I don't mean begin construction of a fence or trail. This baseline will be imaginary.

To do this, take a bearing off a prominent landmark while standing in your camp by holding your compass level at waist height and pointing the direction-of-travel arrow at the landmark. Rotate the compass housing until the red end of the magnetic compass needle is centered (boxed) within the orienting arrow. Your bearing can be read in degrees at the center index point—where the compass housing meets the direction-of-travel arrow on the compass baseplate. Write this bearing down. It and the line of sight you just took have become your baseline (Figure 5-4).

So off you go, merrily exploring the desert terrain. The time comes to return to camp. Set your compass so that your baseline bearing is at the index point. Point the direction-of-travel arrow at the landmark you sighted off earlier that day and begin walking to the right or left until you have once again centered the magnetic compass needle within the orienting arrow. You're now back on the baseline. Of course, the question now arises: Which way do you

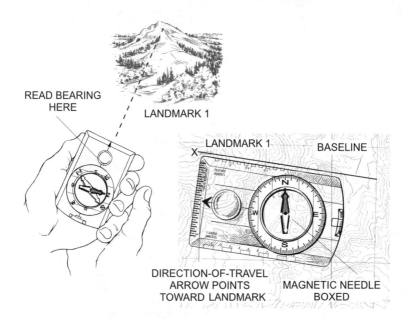

READ BEARING
HERE

LANDMARK 1

LANDMARK 1   BASELINE

X

DIRECTION-OF-TRAVEL
ARROW POINTS
TOWARD LANDMARK

MAGNETIC NEEDLE
BOXED

Figure 5-4 Making a Baseline. Orient map. Hold compass level and sight to landmark. Rotate compass housing and box magnetic needle with orienting arrow. Place compass edge on landmark sighted. Rotate compass while leaving edge on landmark until needle is boxed with orienting arrow. Draw line from landmark. This is a made baseline.

turn on the baseline? Well, if you were smart, you aimed off as described above, ending up on the baseline closer to the landmark so that you know you'll have to follow a back bearing from the landmark to return to camp along the baseline bearing (Figure 5-5).

You can eliminate the worry of having to aim off by adding a second baseline to the mix. Before you leave camp, establish a bearing toward a second easily recognizable landmark and write that bearing down. What you're banking on here is the fact that two straight lines can intersect in only one place (Mr. Frumplemeyer's ninth-grade geometry class covered this if you had been paying attention). This comes into play once you've arrived back at your first baseline. If you have a map and know where the camp is on the map, you can quickly determine which way you should head. First, orient the map. Next, draw the first baseline on the map so that it becomes visible, not imaginary. Now hold your compass level at waist height and point the direction-of-travel arrow at the

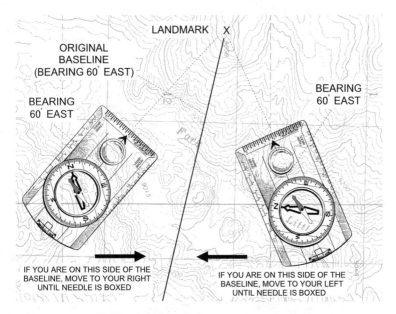

LANDMARK X

ORIGINAL
BASELINE
(BEARING 60° EAST)

BEARING
60° EAST

BEARING
60° EAST

IF YOU ARE ON THIS SIDE OF THE
BASELINE, MOVE TO YOUR RIGHT
UNTIL NEEDLE IS BOXED

IF YOU ARE ON THIS SIDE OF THE
BASELINE, MOVE TO YOUR LEFT
UNTIL NEEDLE IS BOXED

Figure 5-5 Using a Baseline.

second landmark. Rotate the compass housing until the red end of
the magnetic compass needle is centered (boxed) within the orienting arrow. Your bearing can be read in degrees at the center index
point—where the compass housing meets the direction-of-travel
arrow on the compass baseplate. Taking care not to move the map,
place one edge of the compass baseplate directly on the second
landmark, with the direction-of-travel arrow pointing from the
baseline toward the landmark. Now, without moving the compass
housing or moving the map in any way, pivot the compass around
the landmark point until the red end of the magnetic compass needle is centered (boxed) within the orienting arrow. Draw a line,
either in pencil or in your imagination, along the edge of the baseplate until it intersects with the baseline you're standing next to.
Your location on the baseline is where the two lines intersect. You
should now know which way to turn to get back to your camp
(Figure 5-6).

What if you don't have a map? Hold your compass level at waist
height and point the direction-of-travel arrow at your second landmark. Rotate the compass housing until the red end of the magnet-

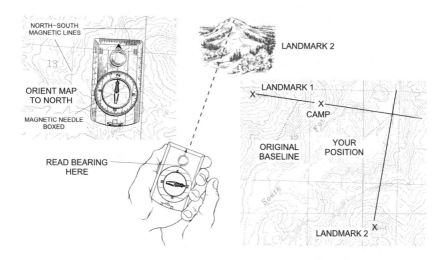

Figure 5-6 Using Two Made Baselines. Orient map. Hold compass level and sight to landmark. Rotate compass housing and box magnetic needle with orienting arrow. Place compass edge on landmark sighted. Rotate compass while leaving edge on landmark until needle is boxed with oriented arrow. Draw line from landmark. Repeat for second baseline.

ic compass needle is centered (boxed) within the orienting arrow. Read the bearing. Compare it with the bearing you wrote down when you sighted off this landmark from camp. Now move to the right or the left on your baseline and take another bearing off the second landmark. Compare it again to the bearing you wrote down. The closer your bearing is to the bearing you wrote down, the closer you are to camp, which means that's the direction you should head.

Pinpointing Your Position: Triangulation

It's important to realize that even with the best navigator and the best handheld compass, error still manages to creep into the mix. On average, each bearing may be off anywhere from 1 to 4 degrees, depending on many factors that can influence the outcome. This means that if you really want to establish an exact location, or as close to exact as you're going to get, you'll need to establish not one, not two, but three baselines. Where those three baselines intersect is your location on the map. Establishing your absolute position fix using triangulation will be much more effective if you can select landmarks that are relatively near you and as spread out as possible around the points of the compass.

First, orient the map. Then hold your compass level at waist height and point the direction-of-travel arrow at the first landmark. Rotate the compass housing until the red end of the magnetic compass needle is centered (boxed) within the orienting arrow. Your bearing can be read in degrees at the center index point—where the compass housing meets the direction-of-travel arrow on the compass baseplate. Taking care not to move the map, place one edge of the compass

Figure 5-7 Triangulation. Orient map. Hold compass level and sight to landmark. Rotate compass housing and box magnetic needle with orienting arrow. Place compass edge on landmark sighted. Rotate compass while leaving edge on landmark until needle is boxed with orienting arrow. Draw line from landmark. Repeat process. Your location is where lines intersect.

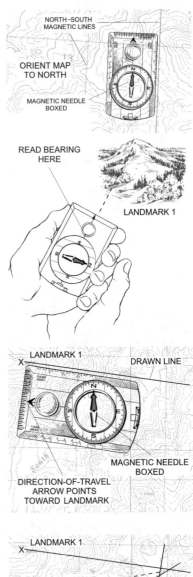

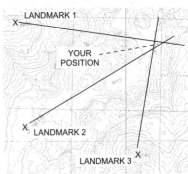

baseplate directly on the landmark, with the direction-of-travel arrow pointing toward the landmark. Now, without moving the compass housing or moving the map in any way, pivot the compass around the landmark point until the red end of the magnetic compass needle is centered (boxed) within the orienting arrow. Draw a line in pencil along the edge of the compass's baseplate. Repeat the steps with a second and third landmark. The area or triangle bounded by all three lines will be the area in which you are located. The farther away the landmarks, you sight off, the larger the triangle. The closer the landmarks, the smaller the triangle and the more accurate your fix (Figure 5-7).

Ded Reckoning

I once thought that this referred to navigating from the hip because all your other resources were exhausted. Then I began sailing. That was when I learned that the term is based in nautical history (ancient mariners relied on this method to find their way across uncharted waters) and refers to reckoning by logical deduction. The word *dead* actually came from a contraction of *deduction*—ded. So, in reality, this is "ded (deduction) reckoning," which makes much more sense to me.

Ded reckoning isn't as accurate as other forms of navigation, but it will suffice, especially in those circumstances when the identifiable land features are few and far between. You must start with an established point of origin or a fix. Mark this point on the map. From this point, establish a compass heading and then stick to it for a measurable distance. Military personnel are taught to silently count off the number of steps they have walked; and that's as good a method as any. Consider that for the average human, each normal walking step is approximately 2 ½ feet long. So if you count one for every time your right foot hits the ground, you can tally up 5 feet of distance covered. If you want to be really accurate, put a pebble in a pocket for every one hundred times your right foot hits the ground. Each pebble in your pocket will then equal about 500 feet.

Estimate your second established point on the map by counting pebbles and multiplying by 500. Since 1 mile equals 5,280 feet, you can use the map's scale to estimate how far on the map you have traveled. Mark the second point on the map. That point has been established by ded reckoning. For obvious reasons, the longer the distance you cover, the more likely you are to make a larger error. If you decide to change direction at this second point, establish another compass heading and begin counting steps anew. Each time you change direction, establish another ded reckoning point on the map. In this way you can roughly chart your course and position.

Another useful application for ded reckoning doesn't involve a map at all—only your compass and an accurate measurement of time or distance. Say you have no map, but want to head out from point A to explore the surrounding terrain and still have a reasonable shot at arriving back at point A again. The terrain is featureless, so establishing a bearing as a baseline is out of the question. What do you do? From point A, head out at an established bearing, making sure you write it down so that you don't forget it. Either keep time with your watch or measure your steps as outlined above. When it comes time to change direction, mark it down as point B. Record the elapsed time or steps counted between points A and B, establish your new bearing, and then remember to write the new bearing down. Repeat these steps every time you change direction until you decide it's time to head back to point A again. To be precise, you must first establish a distance scale so that you can accurately, draw a map using your recorded elapsed time or distance measurements. For instance, you might establish that every fifteen minutes or 250 steps represents ¼ inch. Beginning with point A either drawn on a piece of paper or scratched into the dirt, measure your elapsed distance to point B using the same bearing you followed earlier in the day. From point B, place the bearing to point C on the index line of the compass, point the direction-of-travel arrow toward point C, and once again measure the correct distance covered. Repeat this until you've plotted your course on the ground or on the paper with one last leg left unplotted—the leg returning you to point A. Pointing your direction-of-travel arrow at point A from the last point plotted—say point L—turn the dial and center (box) the magnetic needle with the orienting arrow. Read the bearing at the index point—this is the bearing you will follow to get back to A. Keep in mind that you've been using

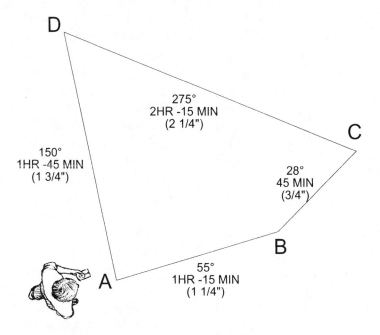

D

275°
2HR -15 MIN
(2 1/4")

C

150°
1HR -45 MIN
(1 3/4")

28°
45 MIN
(3/4")

B

A

55°
1HR -15 MIN
(1 1/4")

Figure 5-8

ded reckoning, so don't expect to be exact. If you were careful, though, you should come very close (Figure 5-8).

Estimating Distance

Estimating distance is useful to paddlers, hunters, or any adventurers who may be contemplating a paddle or trek to a distant peak, island, or point in the desert that appears deliciously close. Remember, my friends, things are not always as they appear. Objects will assuredly look closer than they are if the atmosphere is brilliantly clear or if they're viewed across flat, open terrain such as sand, water, or snow. If you're carrying a range finder, you're home free. Chances are, though, that you've opted to save the expense, weight, and bulk of this item—which leaves you to estimate.

One tried-and-true method involves winking. Ever notice that if you alternately open one eye and then the other, objects you are gazing at appear to move back and forth? Well, you can use this to your advantage, providing you know the width in miles or feet of

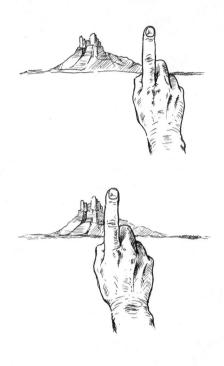

the object from which you're estimating your distance. For paddlers, this involves finding out how wide a distant point or island is. For hunters or hikers, you'll need to know how wide a plateau or mountain is. With one eye closed, extend your arm and hold up one finger. Using the open eye, sight the finger to the opposite side of the object (left eye to right corner or right eye to left corner). Now close that eye and open the other to look at the same finger. Estimate how far across the object your finger appeared to jump—one eighth, one quarter, one half, one?

Figure 5-9

Now divide the width of the object into the fractions represented by your finger observation. For example, if your finger appeared to jump halfway across an object you know to be 1 mile wide, then the movement equaled 0.5 mile. The formula for establishing distance is to multiply that distance by 10. That means that 10 x 0.5 = 5; you're approximately 5 miles from the object (Figure 5-9).

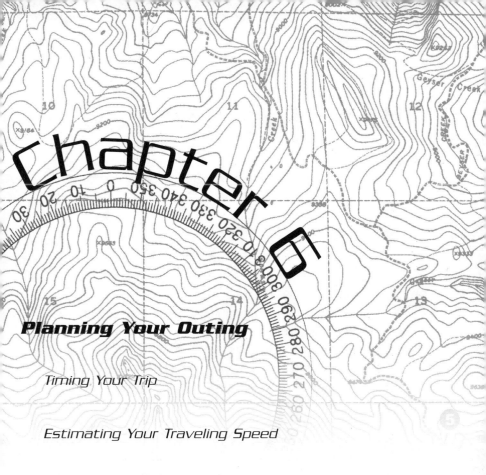

chapter 6

Planning Your Outing

Timing Your Trip

Estimating Your Traveling Speed

Finding the Trail and Staying on Course

Picking a Route When Your Life Depends on It

Planning Your Outing

Always plan your hike and hike your plan. This advice goes for any adventure, whether a hike or not. If you get into trouble and you left an itinerary of your trip with a friend, rescuers should be able to find you easily. When I taught outdoor skills courses for Adventure 16 in southern California, I mandated that all of my students learn to leave detailed itineraries with a family member, close friend, or responsible neighbor. For obvious reasons, it's better for you if this person has a vested interest in your safe return—either because they like you or because you owe them a lot of money. What you'll leave with them is as follows: name and emergency contact numbers for everyone with whom you're traveling; your vehicle description and license number; your anticipated return time; your route and intended campsites, complete with a map with the route highlighted if possible; an alternate route should weather or something else alter your plans; and the person to contact to initiate a rescue if you are overdue. Don't forget to notify your friend when you do return so that they don't worry and, most important, so that a rescue team doesn't get called out when you're sitting safely in front of a hot meal at home.

Timing Your Trip

Getting stuck out for the night is not, strictly speaking, the same as getting lost, but both typically occur because you've miscalculated either trip distance or trip time, or perhaps both. Learning to accurately estimate how long a particular hike will take you is an essential part of the navigator's planning game (especially with day trips, since you probably won't be carrying any camping gear). If you're in the habit of trying to play it thin so you arrive—you hope— back at your camp or your car the second it gets absolutely dark, expect to get burned from time to time. It's always better to plan conservatively. A simple formula applies to almost all circumstances.

Once you've decided where you want to go and when, the most important thing to determine is the time it's slated to get dark on that day. Depending on the terrain and the season, darkness can settle over you like a blanket in just five minutes (in mountainous jungle during the monsoon) or in half an hour (on the beach in the summer). Any local newspaper has sunrise and sunset information. Then, by taking note of when you plan to begin hiking, paddling, or skiing, you can calculate the window of time you have. If you start at noon and dusk falls at 6:00 P.M. you have six hours of daylight.

When estimating how much time a trek will take, keep in mind that, for the majority of outings, you're going to have far more energy at the beginning of the outing and far less in reserve toward the end. This means that if you start at noon and it gets dark at 6:00, it's best not to wait until 3:00 to charge down the trail more rapidly, hoping to get all the way to your destination and back to the car that day—in the daylight. Better to turn around at 2:00 or 2:30 and allow for a slower pace. Time estimates can get iffy, for instance, when the hike out is virtually all uphill. While you might figure that going downhill will be much faster, the pounding your knees and ankles will take, coupled with your increased fatigue, can sap the life out of even the sturdiest limbs. I always estimate that it will take me one and a half times longer to return from a destination than it took me to get there, and I plan accordingly.

Of course, not all trips proceed according to plan, and that's the beauty of adventuring. What this means, however, is that there will be times when it's probably prudent to turn around before reaching your destination—unless you want to hike in the dark. Knowing when to turn around involves knowing not so much what time it is—although that's useful, too—but how much sunlight is

Figure 6-1

left in the day. Although you may have planned well, perhaps you overlooked the fact that the last 2 miles of the hike back will be along the bottom of the canyon, and that day's light will be chased away from the canyon's depths long before the sun actually sets. So how do you estimate when the sun will disappear behind a ridge and twilight will settle in? By using your eyes and hands. While I realize that not all hands are the same size, this trick serves to roughly estimate time no matter how large your digits are. Look toward the sun, though not directly at it, and hold you hand an arm's length away. Line up the bottom of your pinkie (your fourth finger) with the top of the visible horizon (the top of the canyon wall or a distant ridge, for example). Every four fingers up from the horizon toward the sun account for approximately one hour. So if you hold both your hands out, with one hand on top of the other, and the sun is sitting just above the index finger of your top hand, you can be fairly sure that you have two hours of sunlight left in the day (Figure 6-1).

Estimating Your Traveling Speed

Hitting the Trail at the Speed of . . . Well . . . a Slow-Moving Rock, Perhaps?

Estimating your rate of travel is essential when determining how long you'll need to traverse a particular route. It's no fun planning a three-day hike and then finding you're only halfway home, out of fuel, and out of food on the third day. In general, travel times should be estimated as follows—although keep in mind that you or someone in your group may hike a little faster or even slower. Always hike at the comfort pace of the slowest member of your group.

● Hiking in boots on level ground with a light load and moderate elevation gain—3 to 4 miles per hour.

● Hiking in boots at 6,000 feet of elevation or higher with some hills—3 to 4 miles per hour.

● Hiking in boots bushwhacking or traveling cross-country without the benefit of trails—1.5 to 2 miles per hour.

● Hiking in boots with steep climbing up ridges and mountainsides—0.5 to 1 mile per hour

● Hiking in snowshoes on open terrain with gentle ups and downs—2 to 3 miles per hour.

● Trail running on level ground with a light load and moderate elevation gain—6 to 8 miles per hour

● Trail running at 6,000 feet of elevation or higher with moderate elevation gain and loss—5 to 7 miles per hour.

According to the U.S. Army, the following way is a good method to gauge hiking speed. If you're female and walk between twenty and twenty-one steps every ten seconds, or are male and walk between sixteen and seventeen steps every ten seconds, you're traveling at approximately 3 miles per hour. Stepping out at twenty-seven to twenty-eight steps every ten seconds as a female or twenty to twenty-one steps every ten seconds as a male means you're blazing down the trail at approximately 4 miles per hour. Of course, knowing your estimated speed is one thing; using it to determine how long it will take you to get from point A to B is yet another. For that, you have to factor in elevation gain and loss. Although conservative, most experts suggest adding one hour of time for every 1,000 feet of elevation gain. So to estimate how long your hike is going to take, determine your hike length, elevation gain, and estimated speed of travel. Assuming you hike at 4 miles per hour, a 4-mile hike with 2,000 feet of elevation gain might take you as long as three hours.

Finding the Trail and Staying on Course

How do you know if you're on the right trail or not? Trails are marked in many different ways throughout the country. Blazes, diamonds, or dotted Is carved into a tree about 6 to 8 feet off the ground are common. So are painted blazes or metal plates nailed to a tree. These identifiable trail markers are placed on both sides of the tree and at regular intervals so that you'll be able to spot the next blaze within a few feet of leaving the last one. Following blazes comes with a caveat, however—trees fall or get burned. Sometimes, unthinking backwoods travelers carve their own blazes to help them find their way back to the original route, confusing the matter. You have to use your head and keep a sharp eye out. On occasion, finding the next blaze involves a little sleuthing. Don't panic and, above all, don't just head out blindly along a treadway because it "looks like a trail." Remember that animals walk in the woods, too, and the trails they leave often resemble human foot-paths.

When the track heads above the tree line or through open and treeless areas like deserts or vast plains, trails often are marked with "ducks" or cairns—piles of rocks. Sometimes, in challenging terrain where route finding is a matter of life and death, cairns have been replaced by 5-foot-high wands covered with reflective tape or paint. The Mount Washington area in New Hampshire and Mount Katahdin in Maine are two such areas.

Picking a Route When Your Life Depends on It

Navigational Challenges in Various Terrain

Jungle: Thinking of attempting to track a straight line? Hah! Forget it. The jungle and many rain forests are so dense that you'll have to make use of wildlife paths, ridgelines, streams, dry riverbeds, or established human trails. You'll find that all of the above have one thing in common—they thread their way through the dense understory by running along the bottom of or parallel to the valley floors. This is fine as long as your intended route of travel is going the same way, but more often than not, it isn't. In the jungle perhaps more than anywhere else, it's essential to be skilled in the use of the compass so that you can snake your way around obstacles, along valleys, and over low ridges while still maintaining a semblance of your intended course. Landmarks, if you can see them, will become extremely valuable. Travel during the day and get off any established path at night; animals—frequently predators—cruise along these same trails. If you select a trail, try to pick one that's heading up and out of the valley floor as opposed to meandering along it. Trails that follow valley floors are often overgrown, will more likely involve trickier stream crossings, and will generally be muckier. If you're really in doubt about which way to head, the tried-and-true recommendation of following the nearest watercourse downstream is a good one. Eventually, waterways will lead to human habitation, although be prepared to follow a meandering course that might take you twice as long to cover the same ground you would have covered had you attempted a more direct course of navigational route finding.

Desert: Although maps of the desert regions in the United States are fairly accurate, such is not the case internationally. In order to get to a location where you have a hope of finding human life and preserving your own, it's essential that you know, with reasonable certainty, where you are now so that you can make an educated guess about your direction of travel. If you have no idea where you are now, a map becomes useless, and heading off in any direction is, at best, a roll of the dice. If you're in a survival situation because of a broken-down vehicle and have no idea where you are, it might be best to stay put. Officials who provide information to those traveling into the Australian Outback mandate that you never leave your vehicle: It's far easier for a rescue team to find a vehicle than a person on the move. Should you decide that moving is in your best interests, then travel only in the early morning or late evening, when the sun won't sap the very life from your limbs. Leave positive instructions with your vehicle indicating your direction of travel. If animal trails exist and they're heading in your desired direction of travel, use them. Avoid the temptation to follow watercourses or dry streambeds unless their direction matches the heading you need to follow. Many desert watercourses meander only to depressions or dry lakes inland. However, if the watercourse you come across is full of water and you're in the desert, you should strongly consider staying put—water is life! Pick your way around dunes to conserve valuable energy; the walking is typically easier and the footing firmer in the valleys between dunes. Keep checking and double—checking your heading to be sure you're on course. And whenever possible, use distant landmarks to keep your travels from drifting right or left of your intended destination.

Arctic: This is the one time when you need to forget the advice about hiking downstream to find your way to human habitation. A waterway flowing in a northerly direction will likely lead you away from humans, not toward them. In the winter valley floors are often the easiest places to navigate, since they're somewhat sheltered from the wind that sweeps across the ridges, and the snow has most likely covered any areas choked by underbrush. Always question your compass—being so close to the magnetic pole can mess with a compass's accuracy—and back up your navigational decisions and headings with celestial observation and a sundial or watch (as described in chapter 4) or a GPS. Navigating over vast areas of smooth and often featureless snow can also be exhausting and disorienting.

Coastline: It certainly won't be a straight course, but your route will be an unmistakable one if you choose to follow a coastline. Be aware that any coastal travel will likely involve sweeping winds with driving sand, loose rocks, slippery shores, shifting sands, impassable cliffs, and swampy terrain at river mouths. For those times when you have to head inland to negotiate an impassable feature, be sure to take careful and accurate bearings so that you won't waste valuable time and energy beating around the underbrush trying to find your way back to the coast and the path leading down to the beach on the other side of the cliff or swamp.

Snow: Route finding can become a nightmare in the winter if you get off course and aren't paying close attention to landmarks. This is because many of the usual baselines such as trails, fence lines, and fire roads are buried under a deep blanket of snow. Trail blazes, too, are often buried. In addition, estimating height and distance gets harder, since contours are rounded off and depressions are filled in. Keeping dry can be a challenge because marshes, lakes, and even small streams are covered by snow and ice—but often not deeply enough to hold your weight. What appears to be the quickest route may not be the safest. Always err on the side of caution and work your way around suspect areas. It's essential that you travel with your map and compass always handy. Make fastidious note of each and every recognizable landmark and your position in relationship to it, and find that point on the map, too. Avoid steep slopes that could spell avalanche danger. Keep in mind that, if your route takes you across streams or rivers, the safest time to cross them via a snow bridge will be in the early-morning hours when they're most likely to be frozen solidly. Watch out for warming trends, which can spell disaster. That stream you're planning to cross could turn into a raging flood in only a short time if a warming trend and rain trigger snowmelt.

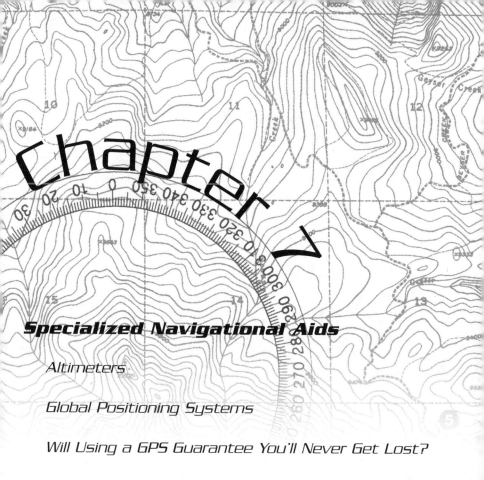

Chapter 7

Specialized Navigational Aids

Altimeters

Global Positioning Systems

Will Using a GPS Guarantee You'll Never Get Lost?

Specialized Navigational Aids

Altimeters

Can Altimeters Be Used as Navigational Tools?

You bet! Altimeters are very useful additions to your navigational system. They're also a worthwhile tool to help forecast weather changes and estimate elevation loss and gain. Pocket altimeters measure and then convert barometric pressure into altitude readings, even if it's dark or you're completely fogged in. By constantly registering your present elevation, an altimeter can be useful in determining when you've reached a given elevation and, consequently, a contour line on a topographic map. That information can then be used to guide you along that contour and elevation to your eventual destination—minimizing energy-wasting searching for the "camp I know is here somewhere!"

The best altimeters are temperature compensated so that temperature fluctuations won't affect the reading too much. To be really useful, however, an altimeter must have measurable increments of no more than 50 feet, or even less, and be accurate to within 100 feet. If you think that you'll be rough on your altimeter, then an electronic one such as the Brunton SHERPA or wrist-top Suunto Vector computer watch will best suit your needs. These are also easier to read and use. For greatest accuracy, a mechanical altimeter with geared movement is the choice. Mechanical altimeters have one distinct advantage over electronic ones: They have no batteries to fail, making them the best choice for extended cold-weather use.

One last word of advice. Since an altimeter registers barometric changes, it will "adjust" altitude readings as the barometric pressure rises and falls, even though the instrument itself may remain at a constant altitude. You'll be wise to learn to recalibrate your altimeter on a regular basis using known points of elevation as you pass over them—in fact, your altimeter will quickly become useless weight unless you regularly recalibrate it.

Using the Altimeter, Practically Speaking

Remember when I spoke of baselines in the earlier chapters? Well, if you're on a baseline, or come across a baseline during your travels, you can use it and your altimeter to confirm your position. For example, the visibility is dropping as you proceed up the ridge toward camp, just below the summit. You can no longer sight off the summit and are becoming unsure of your location on the mountain. You are, however, hiking next to a stream, and you can pinpoint its location on the map. That stream is a baseline. If you think about it, each contour line as you proceed up the mountain is also a baseline, since as the stream flows downhill, it intersects with each contour only once. You whip out your altimeter, knowing you recently calibrated it to a known elevation, and read your altitude— 9,260 feet. Your finger traces a line up the creek to elevation 9,260 feet and, presto, there you are.

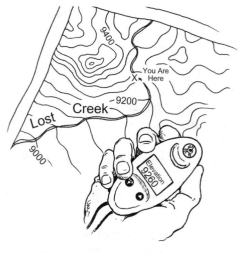

Figure 7-1

Global Positioning Systems

The Global Positioning System (GPS) is made up of a network of twenty-four satellites that orbit the earth twice a day transmitting

Figure 7-2

precise time and position information. With a handheld GPS
receiver, you can determine your location anywhere on Earth.

A GPS receiver works by listening to the signal of three or more
satellites. Then by measuring the time interval between the trans-
mission and the reception of a satellite signal, it can calculate the
distance between you and the satellite. Using the distance measurements of at least three satellites and some fancy math footwork
known as algorithms, the GPS establishes an accurate position fix.
Three satellites must be acquired for the GPS to accurately display
longitude and latitude, and four satellites must be acquired to add
elevation to the mix. Keep in mind that since the U.S. Department
of Defense controls the signals going out to civilian receivers—and
that it intentionally varies the signal in a process called Selective
Availability—the horizontal accuracy of a GPS ranges from 40 feet
to 327 feet. Altitude or vertical accuracy is less, varying between
327 feet and 510 feet. This means you shouldn't plan on using your
GPS as an altimeter.

Why Would You Want a GPS?

A GPS is an ideal tool for those times you're adventuring in relatively featureless areas such as the desert or vast snowfields, or when visibility is reduced to almost nil because of overcast and fog. With a GPS you can determine your exact location on the map with a simple press of a button; you can enter a location from the map into memory and the GPS will help guide you there; or you can store information in the GPS as you travel so that it can help guide you back.

In my opinion, being able to turn to a GPS to establish your exact position, no matter what the weather, is perhaps its most valuable feature. However, the system is a long way from being the magic wand you wave to always get home safely. High mountains, deep canyons, dense forests, and jungle canopy will all obscure the signals a GPS relies on, making the unit useless.

There is also the hidden danger that the power of GPS can lull you into a false sense of security. Even with a GPS, you would be foolhardy to venture far afield without being skilled in map and compass navigation techniques. What if the batteries die, or you drop the receiver, or the antenna breaks, or you drop it in a lake? Without a GPS, could you determine where you are and how to head for home using just a map and compass? If your answer is anything less than a firm and emphatic *"Absolutely no problem!"* you might want to reevaluate your approach and brush up on your navigational skills—by rereading this book, for starters.

Does a GPS Have Any Advantages over a Compass?

Actually, yes. Several, in fact. First, a compass can help you establish your position only if you have two or more visible and readily identifiable landmarks to work with. A GPS will tell you your position (within a 327-foot diameter) even if there are no visible landmarks, such as in a forest, during a whiteout, in a fog, or in terrain where the features all seem the same.

Also, as you've learned in the previous chapters, even while following a compass bearing it's possible to deviate to the left or right of the desired direction of travel if you're not careful. Since compass errors are cumulative, this can result in being off course by a significant distance. With a GPS, as long as your destination waypoint is entered, you'll be able to determine with a push of a button the correct bearing to follow to that waypoint.

When you're working around obstacles such as lakes or mountains with a compass, you'll have to estimate the distance and bearing you're traveling so that you can calculate how far you must return once you're around the obstacle to put yourself back on your original route. This is part calculation, part guesstimation. No such problem for a GPS. Simply work around the obstacle and then ask the unit to provide you with a new bearing to your destination waypoint.

What Features Do You Need in a GPS?

Most GPS receivers allow you to display information in either longitude-latitude, Universal Transverse Mercator (the UTM grids that many Bureau of Land Management and other survey maps use), or military grid. Some, such as the Trimble, display actual map quadrant names and then give inch measurements to help you locate yourself on the listed map. At a minimum your GPS should support both UTM and longitude-latitude grids, because with those two grids you'll be able to use the GPS anywhere in the world.

Route and Goto functions are essential. The Route function allows you to program up to ten waypoints (some units allow even more); it then automatically switches from waypoint to waypoint as you hike along your route, without you even having to touch a button. The Goto function also guides you but in a single application only, meaning that you have to enter the next waypoint into the system manually each time.

Steering is perhaps the most useful tool your GPS offers, if you're willing to hike with your GPS on all the time, because a GPS can't calculate direction if you're standing still. While a compass simply points you in the direction you need to go, a GPS in Goto or Route mode will not only direct you toward your next waypoint but also tell you how far you've traveled, how far you have to go, if you've wandered off course and how to get back, and when you've reached your destination.

Personally, I use my GPS to establish a bearing, which it easily does when in either the Route or the Goto mode. A simple press of a button and my bearing to the next waypoint is displayed. It's a simple matter for me to then turn off my GPS (or place it in battery-save mode if I'm planning to use it again soon), whip out my compass, set the bearing, center (box) the orienting arrow, and hike off in the direction my direction-of-travel arrow points. I must admit that I also really enjoy using the distance function to estimate how much farther I have to go—as the crow flies, of course.

Some GPS units now display actual digitized maps, although the detail is far from ideal. You'll also want a light so you can use your GPS at night, a lithium battery backup so you don't lose all your data when your AA batteries need replacing, a housing that's both durable and weatherproof, and enough memory to store at least 200 waypoints (although 500 or more is best).

The pricier the GPS, the more features it offers—up to complete personal computer interface for uploading and downloading navigational information.

Can a GPS Calculate Traveling Speed While It Keeps You on Course?

Yes, as long as you're willing to burn battery power and keep the GPS out, on, and with a clear view of the sky above—which means holding the unit at arm's length if you intend to hike. Not exactly a practical use.

Real-time navigation complete with the alarms and arrows to keep you on course is pretty neat, but unless you're flying, driving, or boating, it isn't critical information. Still, I must admit that I enjoy the real-time navigation capability of my GPS when I'm mountain biking, which is why some companies offer bike mounts for their units. However, for the backcountry on foot or ski the GPS is best used by turning it on and off intermittently to establish position fixes and obtain your next bearing. And this is why the new twelve-channel receivers are so valuable, because from the time you turn them on to the time they establish a new fix takes mere seconds.

What Advantages Does a Twelve-Channel Receiver Offer?

In the early days most GPS buyers were led to believe that they would experience immediate and reliable navigational information when they turned on a GPS—and most became very disillusioned. Part of the problem stemmed from the fact that the early and cheaper GPS units relied on multiplexing receivers. These receivers used one or two channels to track satellites, find a satellite, lock on to it, read it, then release that satellite to find the next. Since a GPS needs a minimum of three satellites to achieve a two-dimensional position fix and at least four to achieve location and elevation (a three-dimensional fix), a multiplexing GPS had to piece together and then average navigational information. It also typically experienced many problems maintaining satellite contact, especially in marginal conditions such as in canyons, under trees, or near one or two tall obstacles. Unless the area was absolutely clear all around, GPS satellite lock-on was less than reliable. In many cases, even if you did get a reading, it would take up to fifteen minutes, hence the inside joke that to take a reading, you'd best bring out the chairs and a snack.

Enter the twelve-channel or parallel-channel receiver. Still priced at $300 or under, these receivers use each channel to individually lock on to and hold a satellite. Then the four best signals are used to provide accurate, reliable information that's as close to instantaneous as possible. Although some manufacturers continue to offer multiplexing receivers, I advise you firmly against buying one—they're simply not worth it! •

Will Using a GPS Guarantee You'll Never Get Lost?

Yeah, right, and I'll soon be the King of Siam. The GPS is only a tool, and it depends on you making proper use of it to ensure navigational accuracy. Every coordinate must be entered correctly, and then every coordinate must be read correctly. It's a mass of numbers and letters that to the untrained eye can appear confusing—and even to the trained eye can under stress seem mystifying. During the 1996 ESPN Extreme Games Adventure Race, each team used a handheld GPS to stay on course over the 360 miles of dense wilderness and swamp, and I had a hoot watching them veer off course time and again. Would it have been easier with a map and compass? Heck no! But the GPS was no guarantee of success either.

Bottom line—the teams that did well were the ones that had the most experience using the tools at their disposal. Want to stay found? Then practice, practice, practice.

Does a GPS Have Any Significant Limitations?

GPS units are electronic, so you have to realize that they're fragile. Even with armored and waterproof housing, they can be damaged by inadvertent bumps and drops on hard and rocky surfaces. Because they're complicated to use, they can lead you astray simply through human error. If you don't want to take the time to learn to use one by studying the manual (they're thick for a reason) and trying it out and practicing with it around home and in familiar environments, then don't buy one, because it won't do you any good. At temperatures that dip below 0 degrees, GPS units tend to lose valuable function or cease to work at all. Ditto temperatures above 110 degrees—although, come to think of it, I cease to work when it gets that hot, too. Finally, GPS receivers are battery powered and as such, they won't work when the battery becomes depleted. Always carry spare batteries with you.

Remember, too, that a GPS gives you only straight-line navigational information. In other words, if you're traveling from point A to point B, the straight-line bearing indicated by the GPS might take you across a swamp or a canyon or through a man-made hazard. Without a map or good map-reading skills, you could get yourself into deep, deep trouble. Even the manufacturers of GPS units stress that without effective map and compass skills, a GPS cannot be used safely or properly.

Will There Ever Be a Single-Unit GPS-Compass-Altimeter?

Frankly, I've wondered the same thing aloud for several years now, and finally someone is listening—Brunton. As we went to press on this second edition, I got word of a new product called the Brunton Multi Navigator System, or MNS (Figure 7-3). It's a twelve-channel GPS with a built-in electronic IntelliCompass that automatically corrects for declination, as well as an electronic altimeter. I haven't yet had an opportunity to test the unit, but I imagine it will be the first of many others like it.

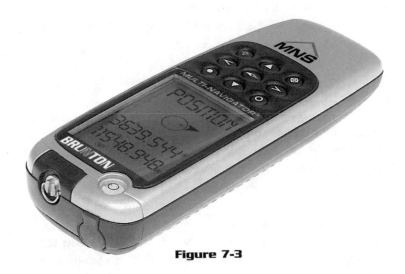

Figure 7-3

Putting Your GPS to Work

Before you use your GPS, you must set it to the local time. Next, determine whether you want it to read in feet, meters, nautical units, or miles for distance measurement; kilometers per hour, miles per hour, or knots for speed measurements. Select the coordinate system you want to use, such as latitude-longitude, UTM, or another one if available. Establish the correct horizontal map datum (printed in the map information box, typically located in the lower left corner of a USGS topographic map) and be sure it's correctly entered into your GPS. Most units allow you to scroll through a wide variety of datum choices to arrive at the correct one. If you select the wrong datum, your bearings could be off by as much as a mile, and certainly in the range of several hundred yards.

Finally, you'll need to initialize your GPS by either turning it on and letting it establish its own coordinate fix (this can take up to fifteen minutes from a cold start) or entering the UTM or latitude-longitude coordinates for where you're now standing, if you know them. Once your GPS has established your current coordinate fix, save it by giving this fix a name and number (for example: Trlhd 1). Now plot your course by entering the coordinates along your route, giving each waypoint a name and a number (I prefer to number sequentially).

As you're moving along, your GPS will give you a current position fix every time you turn it on. From this position fix, you can use the unit to determine a bearing toward and an "as-the-crow-flies" distance to your next waypoint or final destination. Here's where your compass and map skills come in. While the information your GPS is giving you is very valuable, it's almost useless without your basic navigational tools. Once the GPS has given you a bearing, you'll need to turn to your compass to orient yourself to follow that bearing. True, you can use a GPS for this direction finding as long as you leave it on and are in Goto mode, but it takes much longer. Also, while the GPS has given you a bearing to follow and also provided distance information in a straight line, it can tell you nothing about the lay of the land. For all you know it could be pointing you right at a cliff. A quick glance at your map with the bearing information in hand will tell you how easy or difficult the terrain ahead is. Then, using your compass and map together, you can plot a safe and easy route to get you to where you need to be.

What about Declination?

Yes, your GPS can be adjusted for declination, and many will do so automatically depending on the location of the receiver (and, presumably, you). Keep in mind that your GPS reads geographic (true) north; when adjusted to compensate for declination it will show magnetic north. A compass reads magnetic north, and when adjusted to compensate for declination will read geographic (true) north. So, if you adjust both for declination, one will still be reading magnetically and one geographically. I recommend that you leave your GPS in geographic-north mode and adjust your compass for declination—it's far simpler, and no further calculations will be necessary.

Other Practical GPS Applications

Off-Trail Wandering: As you're wandering about the backcountry, a GPS can be a very useful tool in helping you find your way back to a vehicle, tent, or other designated landmark, provided you're meticulous in your approach. I recommend storing a waypoint in your GPS every fifteen minutes, depending on how fast and far you're traveling. Never go more than thirty minutes without storing a waypoint. Be sure to find that waypoint on the map (you *are* carrying one, right? Otherwise there's no point to this exercise . . . we'll just send the search and rescue crews out now). When you're ready to return, turn to the Goto screen on your computer and tell it to Go to the last waypoint you stored. This way, you'll retrace your steps. If you're very good at map reading, you may notice that you could go from, say, waypoint 11 directly to waypoint 3. Again, the GPS will prove very useful, because it will plot the course for you. Then simply whip out your compass and follow the coordinates your GPS gives you.

Planning Your Route at Home: Your GPS can prove very useful for keeping you on the designated route you plotted on the map while at home. Determine the coordinates (in UTM or latitude-longitude) of readily identifiable landmarks and important sites (trailheads, summits, trail junctions, major river crossings, and so on) and enter these into your GPS receiver as waypoints. Be sure to mark each waypoint entry on your map (or in a notepad you carry) for later reference—I prefer on my map. By the first waypoint (where you park your car or where your trip actually begins), mark WP1 (or some other code) on the map, then number all other waypoints sequentially. Be sure the waypoint numbers on the map correspond to the waypoints entered and saved in your GPS. Be extra careful not to establish waypoints that will make it difficult for your GPS to pick up signals, such as at the base of a cliff or in a deep canyon.

When you start your trip, simply turn on your GPS and establish your position. It should match the coordinates you entered for your first waypoint (WP1). Now, using the Goto function, establish the coordinates you need to follow to arrive at WP2, whip out your compass (be sure it's adjusted for declination), and head off the established bearing.

Don't Forget about Selective Availability*: Just because you have a GPS in hand and your friend has given you absolutely accurate coordinates to the food cache doesn't mean you'll find that cache without a little searching. I've taken part in many GPS exer-

---

*Note: As of May 1, 2000, selective availability was turned off. As a result, the accuracy of handheld GPS units has greatly increased from 100-meter positioning accuracy to 10 meters, depending on the type of receiver being used. It should also be noted that the government has control of this system, and during war time selective availability can be turned back on.

cises with search and rescue crews and during basic instruction exercises, and I found great humor in everyone's immediate assumption that if the GPS says the buried treasure is here, it must be so, and if it isn't the treasure has moved. *Wrong*. Because of Selective Availability, you'll arrive within 327 feet in any given direction of a stored coordinate. What does this mean? It means that if you're trying to find a trail junction, a secluded picnic spot, a hidden spring, or a lost person, when your GPS tells you that you've arrived at the given coordinates and you see nothing, set up a search grid around that point to find exactly the location you're seeking. You can either walk around the point your GPS arrived at in ever-widening circles up to a diameter of 327 feet, or you can walk a grid up and down 327 feet each way, spacing your selected route each time by 30 feet. You'll find what you're seeking if you are careful, meticulous, and patient.

Making Sense of GPS Speak

Thanks to the introduction of GPS into our navigational world, you'll encounter new lingo in manuals and instruction books. The following should help you slice through a bit of the confusion.

Azimuth: Another word for bearing.

Coordinate: GPS relies on coordinates, which are nothing more than a series of numbers that indicate on which map and in which grid the position displayed is located. Latitude and longitude and UTM eastings and northings are nothing more than coordinates on a grid.

Course Deviation Indicator (CDI): A function of a GPS receiver that indicates the amount of lateral difference, one way or the other, that a GPS may deviate from a straight-line course between two waypoints.

Course Over Ground (COG): The direction the GPS receiver is actually traveling.

Differential GPS: If your GPS is a differential model, it relies on a method of compensating for Selective Availability to improve its accuracy to within $16\frac{1}{2}$ feet.

ETA (Estimated Time of Arrival): A function of many GPS units that estimates your projected time of arrival at a destination waypoint based on your rate of travel. Keep in mind that this is as the crow flies and can't take into account ups and downs or unexpected direction changes to work around obstacles.

ETE (Estimated Time En Route): A function of many GPS units that estimates how much time you have left to travel before you arrive at a given destination waypoint. Keep in mind that this is as the crow flies and can't take into account ups and downs or unexpected direction changes to work around obstacles.

Grid: A pattern of squares on your map that serve to fix your position. Coordinates provide numbers that allow you to find a horizontal line as well as a vertical one, then follow them to the point of intersection, placing you within that particular grid.

Latitude-Longitude: Latitude lines (horizontal) are parallel to the equator, and longitude lines (vertical) are drawn to connect each pole. Coordinates are measured in degrees, minutes, and seconds.

Map Datum: The reference point from which all maps are drawn. GPS is based universally on a grid for the entire Earth that a GPS can interpret anywhere in the world called WGS-84. Unfortunately, many maps were published before the advent of GPS, so they use different datums. In North America there are two datums: North American Datum 1927 (NAD27) and the North American Datum 1983 (NAD83). Be sure your GPS can interpret the map datums for the areas you'll be in.

Military Grid Reference System: A coordinate system that subdivides the UTM coordinate system by using letter pairs to represent 10-kilometer-by-10-kilometer squares.

RS-232: The standard connection to your computer. This serial port allows your GPS to communicate with your personal computer.

Selective Availability: The intentional distortion of GPS signals received by civilian-grade GPS units to ensure that their position fixes are not as accurate as military and national security fixes. It was turned off on May 1, 2000.

Speed over Ground (SOG): The speed at which the GPS determines it's traveling along its route.

TFF (Time to First Fix): The amount of time it will take your GPS receiver to make its first position fix after it has been in the off position more than a month, lost its memory, or been moved more than 300 miles without an interim fix. Typically, this won't amount to more than fifteen minutes. It's also known as initialization or cold starting.

Two-Dimensional Mode (2D): Only three satellites are being used for a position fix. This is the least accurate of all GPS modes.

Three-Dimensional Mode (3D): At least four satellites are being used for a position fix of estimated altitude as well as position. This is the most accurate GPS mode.

Waypoint: The coordinates of a location that you enter or read on the GPS. Waypoints are stored in your unit's memory and can be recalled with the push of a button.

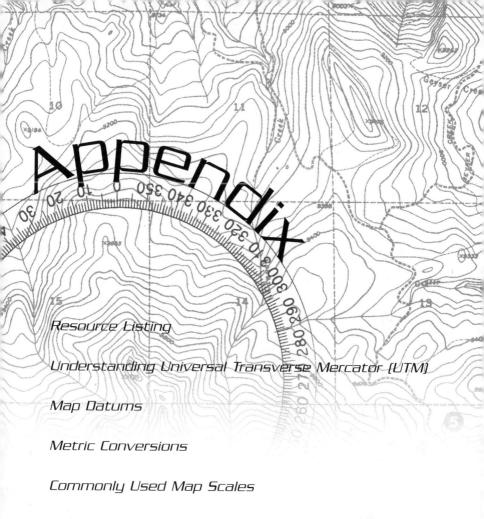

Appendix

Resource Listing

Electronic Compasses
Nexus: (307) 856-6559
Precise Navigation: (415) 903-1499

Handheld GPS Systems
Brunton: (307) 856-6559
Magellan: (909) 394-5000
Trimble: (800) 827-8000
Garmin: (913) 599-1617
Sony: (800) 342-5721
Eagle/Lowrance: (800) 324-1354

Handheld Compasses
Brunton: (307) 856-6559
Silva: (607) 779-2264
Sun: (800) 441-0132
Suunto: (619) 931-6788
Nexus: (307) 856-6559

Maps
U.S. Geological Survey (USGS) (800) USA-MAPS. Topographic maps covering almost all of the United States.

United States Forest Service, Public Affairs Office (202) 205-1760. Maps of all the national forests.

National Park Service (NPS) (202) 208-4747. Maps of all the national parks.

Bureau of Land Management, Public Affairs Office (202) 343-5717. Maps of all the BLM lands.

Canada Map Office (613) 952-7000. Topographic maps for all of Canada and the Northwest Territories.

Map Link (805) 965-4402. One of the best sources of obscure maps for anywhere in the world. If you are heading somewhere and can't find a map, even if it's in the United States, give Map Link a call. Chances are, if a map is in print, this company can locate it for you—for a price, of course.

Trails Illustrated (800) 962-1643. Waterproof and, in my opinion, the most up-to-date topographic maps of our nation's national parks as well as many recreation and wilderness areas.

Tom Harrison Cartography (415) 456-7940. Excellent topographic maps of parks and wilderness areas in California.

Earthwalk Press (701) 442-0503. Topographic maps for western parks and wilderness areas as well as recreational areas in Hawaii.

Appalachian Trail Conference (304) 535-6331. Topographic maps of the Appalachian Trail as it winds its way through the fourteen states.

Wilderness Press (510) 843-8080. Topographic maps that coincide with this publisher's excellent field guides for the Sierra and other areas in California.

DeLorme Mapping (207) 865-4171. Topographic atlases for most of the fifty states. Excellent resource for planning purposes.

Wildflower Productions (415) 282-9112, CD-ROM maps for Yosemite, the San Francisco area, and others. Excellent!

Understanding Universal Transverse Mercator (UTM)

What UTM does:

☉ Divides the globe into sixty zones, each 6 degrees wide.

☉ Zone 1 begins at east/west longitude 180.

☉ UTM in effect peels each zone off the globe and flattens it, making it much easier to project and use on a flat one-dimensional map surface. Since each zone is now distorted, the coordinates are referred to as false coordinates.

☉ Regions above north latitude 84 and below south latitude 80 are too distorted to use, so they're excluded from maps using the UTM grid system.

✪ At no time does UTM designation use a letter system. However, the U.S. Military Grid Reference System (MGRS) does, and sometimes GPS units designate a letter before a UTM grid coordinate to help you know where on the globe the coordinates refer to. MGRS divides each UTM zone horizontally into 8-degree sections; each section is assigned a letter, beginning with C for S80 to S72 and ending with X for N72 to N84. So if the grid coordinate is preceded with a letter, such as N as shown below, you know that the coordinates lie somewhere between the equator and N8 (see Figure A-1).

How UTM Works

Eastings

✪ Every zone is divided down the middle vertically by what's known as a zone meridian. Since each zone is 6 degrees wide and the zone meridian is always the middle longitude line, it's always 3 degrees from either side of the zone. With me so far?

✪ So the zone meridian of zone 2 above would be 171. A zone meridian is always labeled ^{5}00^{000}m.E. Coordinates lie east or west of the zone meridian. If east, the numbers will increase. If west, the numbers will decrease. For example, a coordinate of ^{5}01^{560}m.E lies 1,560 meters east of the meridian. A coordinate of ^{4}85^{500}m.E is (500,000 - 485,500 = 14,500) 14,500 meters or nine miles west of the meridian.

Northings

✪ Northings are measured relative to their position from the equator. The northing value assigned to the equator is ^{0}00^{0000}m.N for coordinates north of the equator and ^{100}00^{0000}m.N for coordinates south of the equator. A coordinate of ^{58}97^{000}m.N above the equator means the point lies 5,897,000 meters (3,665 miles) above the equator. A coordinate of ^{58}97^{000}m.N below the equator lies (10,000,000 - 5,897,000 = 4,103,000) 4,103,000 meters or 2,550 miles south of the equator.

❂ What the above demonstrates is that as you go north, northing values always increase. However, the same number can be used to pinpoint different locations north and south of the equator. Thus it's essential that you indicate if the said coordinate is above or below the equator—one major reason why MGRS is so valuable.

Estimating Distance with UTM

The UTM grid is based upon meter and grid lines that are always 1 kilometer (0.62 mile) apart, making it much easier to estimate distance on a map. UTM coordinates are printed on a map in east–west and north–south positions. Numbers along the right and left side of a map are called northings (indicating the exact position in a north-south relationship). Numbers along the top or bottom of the map are called eastings (indicating the exact position in an east–west relationship).

Making sense of the numbers is quick and easy:

❂ Increasing easting numbers indicate that you're heading east; decreasing mean you're heading west. Increasing northing numbers indicate that you're heading north; decreasing mean you're heading south.

❂ A reading of full UTM positions written along the side of your map might go as follows:

First mark (^{4}35^{000}m.N.), and then second mark (^{4}36^{000}m.N.). What does this mean? The larger numbers (35 and 36) indicate thousands of meters, and since 1,000 meters equals 1 kilometer, the two ticks are 1,000 meters or 1 kilometer apart. The last three numbers are printed smaller and indicate hundreds of meters. If the readings of the marks were (^{4}35^{000}m.N.) and then (^{4}35^{500}m.N.), this would indicate that the ticks were 500 meters or 0.5 kilometer apart.

You need to understand UTM if you plan on working with GPS or on using maps other than those printed by the USGS—the BLM relies on the UTM system heavily. Many guidebooks and directions offered in descriptions give UTM bearings rather than latitude-longitude.

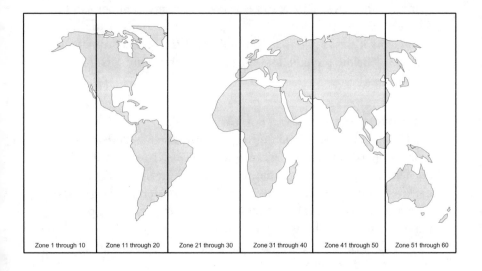

| Zone 1 through 10 | Zone 11 through 20 | Zone 21 through 30 | Zone 31 through 40 | Zone 41 through 50 | Zone 51 through 60 |

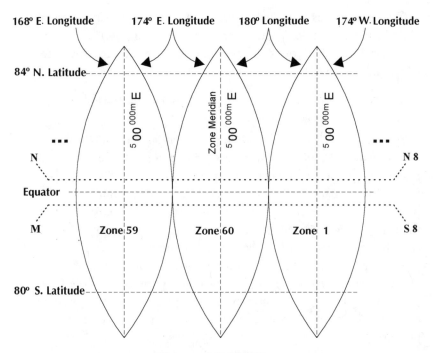

Figure A-1 UTM Zones

Before entering the field with a GPS receiver, the user should understand what a map datum is and how it is used in a GPS receiver.

A datum point is a known reference position from which all other measurements are made. A map datum point is a known location on Earth from which a map is drawn. All countries have drawn maps using a map datum and transformations to make the earth into a flat, usable map of their country. However, not all of the reference positions and transformations are the same in every country.

All GPS receivers use the World Geodetic System 1984, sometimes abbreviated WGS84 or WGS-84 by GPS manufacturers. Use the WGS84 map datum worldwide, but only when a country's map datum is unavailable. It is possible to change map datums in the GPS receiver's setting mode.

North America, including the United States, commonly supports either the North American Datum 1927 (NAD27) or the WGS84 map datum. Check the map for the map datum used to draw it. A United States Department of the Interior Geological Survey (topographic) map almost always uses the NAD27 map datum, and this is described in its legend—see the figure below. If the datum is unknown, use WGS84.

Mapped, edited, and published by the Geological Survey

Control by USGS and USC&GS

Topography by photogrammetric methods from aerial photographs taken 1964. Field checked 1965

Polyconic projection. 1927 North American datum

10,000-foot grid based on Wyoming coordinate system, west zone

1000-meter Universal Transverse Mercator grid ticks, zone 12, shown in blue

Fine red dashed lines indicate selected fence lines

Where omitted, land lines have not been established.

If you travel to other countries and use a GPS receiver, check the map datum the country supports to draw their maps and select the appropriate map datum before saving any positions. If you do not utilize the same map datum that is supported on the map at hand, your saved position could have an error by as much as 1 mile or more.

Following is a small list of just a few map datums.

WGS84-World Geodetic System 1984
   Map datum supported by all GPS receivers
NAD27-North American Datum 1927
   Map datum supported by U.S., Canada, and Mexico
NAD83-North American Datum 1983
   A new map datum the U.S. is currently developing and will be using more often.
AGD84-Australian Geodetic Datum 1984
   Map datum supported by Australia

Some GPS receivers have only a few map datums, and others have over 100 map datums. When buying GPS receivers, check that the receiver will support the map datums you need.

Metric Conversions

1 millimeter (mm) = 0.039 inch
1 inch = 25.4 millimeters (mm)
1 centimeter (cm) = 0.394 inch
1 inch = 2.54 centimeters (cm)
1 meter (m) = 39.37 inches / 3.28 feet / 1.09 yards
1 foot = 0.305 meter (m)
1 yard = 0.914 meter (m)
1 kilometer (km) = 3,281 feet / 0.62 miles
1 mile = 1.61 kilometers (km)
1:15,000 meters scale (most often for orienteering)
1:24,000 scale; 7.5-minute USGS map
1:25,000 meters scale

Commonly Used Map Scales

1:50,000 meters scale
1:62,500 scale; 15-minute USGS map
1:63,360: 1 inch = 1 mile
1:250,000: 120-minute USGS map
(See Appendix Figure A-5)

Azimuth Rings

0-360 degrees - Global/Universal
Quads (4 x 0-90 degrees) Geological/Surveying
Mils (0-6400) - Military = 1 yard at 1,000 yards or 17.777 miles = 1°
Grads (0-400 grads) = European

QUAD

MILS

GRADS

0-360

Figure A-2

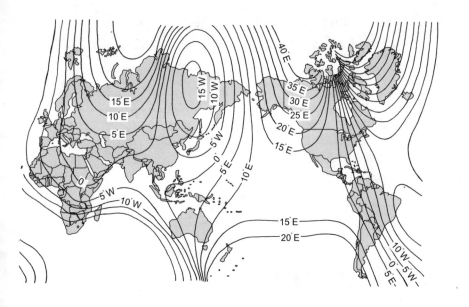

Figure A-3 Magnetic World Variation Chart

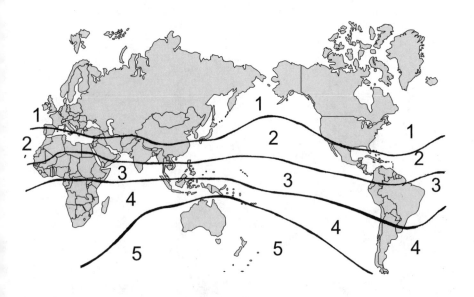

Figure A-4 Magnetic World Balancing Chart

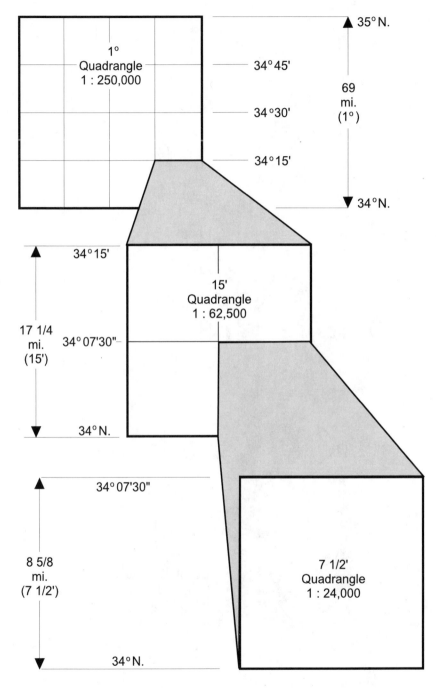

Figure A-5 Map Series Comparison

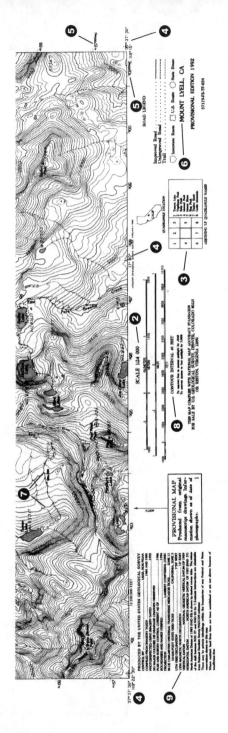

Figure A-6 Topographic maps printed since 1992

Glossary of Terms

Altimeter: An instrument that measures elevation by using barometric (air) pressure.

Azimuth: Same as bearing. Refers to the degree of bearing from your current position to a landmark or destination. Reversing the bearing would be known as back azimuth or back bearing.

Azimuth Ring: See Housing

Back Bearing: The 180-degree opposite of the azimuth or bearing. Also known as back azimuth.

Back-Sighting: What you do when you're establishing a back bearing.

Baseplate: The see-through plate of an orienteering compass onto which the compass housing is mounted.

Bearing: The direction of travel from your current position to a landmark or destination expressed in degrees from 1 to 360. Same as azimuth.

Benchmark: A permanent (as permanent as things can be in this world) object that is either natural or man-made and has a known elevation that can be used as a reference point when navigating.

Boxing the Needle: Placing the red end of the magnetic needle exactly over the red end of the orienting arrow when determining a bearing. Since the orienting arrow is slightly larger than the magnetic needle, we refer to having "boxed" the magnetic needle in. Some books or manuals will refer to this as "red on red" or "centering" the needle.

Cardinal Points: The four main points of direction on a compass are North, 360 degrees; East, 90 degrees; South, 180 degrees; and West, 270 degrees.

Clinometer: A feature found on some compasses that allows the compass to measure vertical angles (such as the slope of a hill). A clinometer can also be used as a level.

Contour Interval: The difference in elevation (height) between one contour line and the next. This interval is expressed in either feet or meters.

Contour Line: Each contour line is comprised of an often irregular closed loop that connects points of equal elevation. The line with a darker shade of brown, typically every fifth line, is called an index contour and usually has the elevation printed on it. Elevations refer to elevation above sea level.

Declination: The difference in degrees between magnetic north (the direction the magnetic needle on a compass points) and true or geographic north (the direction maps are printed toward).

Depression: A natural or man-made hole in the ground that may or may not have a wet bottom. Depressions are shown on topographic maps by a contour line with small hachure marks pointing inward.

Direction-of-Travel Arrow: The arrow engraved or painted onto the front of the baseplate of the compass that is designed to indicate the direction you should hike when a bearing has been established, or the direction you should point the compass to establish a bearing.

Hachure: Short lines used to represent relief features that lie in the direction of the steepest slope.

Housing: The rotating part of the compass that holds the damping fluid and the magnetic needle and has degrees engraved around its edge from 1 to 360. Also known as the azimuth ring.

Index Line: The point at which the direction-of-travel arrow meets the housing and where the degree reading should be read to establish a bearing.

Latitude: The distance in degrees north and south from the equator. These lines run laterally (horizontally) around the globe and parallel to the equator. One minute of latitude equals 1 nautical mile.

Longitude: The distance in degrees east and west from the Prime Meridian established in Greenwich, England. These lines run vertically (lengthwise) around the globe and connect each pole.

Magnetic Lines: Lines drawn onto a topographic map by the user to indicate the direction of magnetic north and to allow the map to speak the same directional language as the compass.

Magnetic North: The geographic region toward which all magnetic needles point. This point is approximately 1,300 miles south of true north and moves slightly each year due to the earth's rotation and the friction created between its solid crust and liquid center.

Map Projection: The process of transforming a round object (the earth) into a flat object (a map) with the least amount of distortion. There is always some distortion caused in this process, which is why grid lines are not perfectly parallel.

Meridian: An imaginary line circling the earth and passing through the geographic poles. All points on any meridian have the same longitude.

Orienteering: Using a map and compass in the field to determine your route of travel. The term has commonly come to refer to a type of competition in which competitors try to navigate across challenging terrain from point to point to arrive at the finish first.

Orienting a Map: Turning the map so that it represents a one-dimensional image that comes as close as possible to exactly paralleling the three-dimensional world you are standing in.

Orienting Arrow: The north–south arrow engraved or painted in red or black into the compass housing. It is slightly wider than the magnetic needle and is used to box or surround the magnetic needle when establishing a bearing.

Orienting Lines: The lines on the bottom of the compass housing that parallel the orienting arrow.

Parallel of Latitude: An imaginary line that circles the earth parallel to the equator. All points on a given parallel have the same latitude.

Position Fix: Sometimes referred to as fixing your position. This means establishing your exact position on a map in terms of a coordinate system such as latitude–longitude or UTM.

Prime Meridian: The meridian that runs through Greenwich, England, at a longitude of 0 degrees. It's used as the position or origin for measurements of longitude.

Prismatic Compass: A compass with a mirror designed to allow you to see both distant objects being sighted and the compass face at the same time.

Protractor: Sometimes built into a compass, this instrument allows you to determine and measure angles in degrees and is most useful when projecting magnetic lines across your map.

Quadrangle: A four-sided section of land bounded by parallels of latitude and meridians of longitude depicted on or by a topographic map. Topo maps are sometimes referred to as quads.

Relief: Changes in terrain.

Relief Shading: A process of shading the map so that it takes on a three-dimensional look. Typically, maps are shaded as if the light source casting the shadow is coming from the northwest.

Scale: The distance between two points on a map as they relate to the distance between those two points on the earth.

Sighting Line: Sometimes called the line of sight, this refers to the imaginary line that you sight along to take your bearing.

True North: Also known as geographic north—the North Pole.

Waypoint: A checkpoint used as a point of reference for GPS.